SERMON SEASONINGS

Collected Stories
to Spice Up
Your Sermons

D1506345

Other books by Ralph Milton

Radio Broadcasting for Developing Nations
The Gift of Story
Through Rose-colored Bifocals
This United Church of Ours
Commonsense Christianity
Is This Your Idea of a Good Time, God?
God for Beginners
Living God's Way
The Family Story Bible
Angels in Red Suspenders

Ralph is also the author of the popular periodical,
Aha!!! the preacher's research assistant,
published bimonthly by Wood Lake Books.

Ralph
Milton

SERMON
SEASONINGS

Collected Stories

to Spice Up

Your Sermons

WOOD
LAKE
BOOKS

Editor: Wendy Smallman
Consulting editor: Jim Taylor
Cover design: Margaret Kyle
Consulting art director: Robert MacDonald

At Wood Lake Books

we practice what we publish, guided by a concern for fairness,
justice, and equal opportunity in all of our relationships
with employees and customers.

Canadian Cataloguing in Publication Data
Milton, Ralph.
 Sermon seasonings

 Includes index.
 ISBN 1-55145-248-0

 1. Milton, Ralph. 2. Homiletical illustrations. I. Smallman,
Wendy D., 1941- II. Title
BV4225.2.M54 1997   251'.08   C97-910045-3

Printing 10 9 8 7 6 5 4 3 2 1

Published by   Printed in Canada by
Wood Lake Books Inc.,   Best Book Manufacturer
10162 Newene Rd. Winfield BC
Canada V4V 1R2

How to use this book

This book represents a collection of writings by Ralph Milton done over many years and for various different reasons. Wendy Smallman went through his work and picked out those stories, anecdotes, thoughts that she felt would be useful to speakers and preachers and resource developers. The material was only updated when not to do so would make it useless.

Each item was given a number of "handles" or "finder words" to make this resource more useful. The first word is in uppercase outline type and it is according to those designations that the items are arranged in the book.

Below them are a number of other "handles" in lowercase. When you look in the index and find a listing in lower case, that means the item has another main designation. For instance, you may find the word "achievement" in lower case, and find the item in question under MARION ANDERSON on page 11.

A word about copyright.

All these materials are copyright. However, if you have purchased a copy of the book, you have our permission to quote in a speech or sermon or meditation. You may also use quotes in a church bulletin or a program. In these cases, please give credit as it feels comfortable, which may only mean that you say something like "Ralph Milton says...."

If you wish to use a quote in a periodical or book, you may do so without charge provided you give full credit to Ralph Milton, the book the material came from, and Wood Lake Books. The name of the source cited in *Sermon Seasonings* is the one you should mention. If you have questions, please phone PERMISSIONS, Wood Lake Books at 250.766.2778 or fax 250.766.2736.

ADVENT

Encouragement	Matthew 3:1-17
Hope	Mark 1:1-11
Miracle	Luke 1:5-24, 39-45, 57-80, 3:1-20

It was right out of Monty Python – this during my summer sabbatical while studying in Israel for six weeks.

It's morning on the Sinai Peninsula. We've climbed the holy Moses mountain and we're on our journey home through the most desolate area in the whole earth. If God wanted to get the children of Israel down to basics, this was the place to do it. This is the wilderness. Rock, rubble, 35 degree heat.

Halfway between nowhere and nowhere, the bus dies. It just quits. I begin to wonder how to word the note which will be crumpled in my mummified hand when they find our desiccated bodies ten years from now.

We stand in the narrow shade of the tour bus. Our Egyptian tour guide smiles, and promptly flags down a taxi which just happened to be coming down the road at that time. He seemed to see nothing unusual in that.

The taxi disappears over the horizon of rock and rubble, I take a disconsolate tug at my bottle of tepid water and again begin composing my famous last words when...now this is true...I didn't make it up...along comes an ice-cream truck. Complete with pictures of ice-cream cones and other goodies all over its pure white exterior.

We assumed it was a mirage until two smiling men got out of the mirage, and asked about our problem. One of them opened the back and offered us...no, not ice cream...they didn't actually have any ice cream...but ice cold water! The other man helped our driver tinker with the engine, and soon our bus was running again.

Advent is the time of standing in the wilderness not wondering whether we'll survive, but feeling quite certain we won't. Along comes John the Baptist driving a taxi that goes for help.

And God's response in sending a baby to Bethlehem, a baby who grows and goes to desiccated desert travelers with a drink of cold, refreshing water, is a lot harder to believe than ice-cream trucks in the Sinai.

But both stories are true.

ADVERTISING

| Attitude | Matthew 6:25-34 | Psalm 8 |
| Self-worth | Luke 12:22-31, 13:10-17 | Genesis 1, 2 |

The advertisers promise but they can't deliver. They can sell you a car or a chicken, but they can't sell a sense of self-worth. And in spite of the fact that we're told, perhaps hundreds of times a day, that we only qualify as humans if we purchase certain products, not one of those products can make us any more human. So the cynicism and the humiliation and depersonalization mount.

Advertisers often argue that they don't create public attitudes. They only reflect what people already believe. That's both true and false. It is true that communication research has established beyond doubt that media mostly reinforce existing attitudes. But it seems to me that if the media consistently reinforce the most destructive attitudes of society, they are in fact degrading it!

AFFIRMATION

Family		
Prayer		
Reassurance		Isaiah 49:15-16a
Security		1 Thessalonians 5:17

My mom told the story often to our kids. "When your dad was a small boy, he'd be out playing in the back yard for hours. Then he'd come running into the house, and he'd leap up into my arms and give me a hug. Then he'd run out and play again. Sometimes he'd almost knock me off my feet."

"Why did he do that, Grandma?"

"I guess he just needed to check in to see if I was still there."

I remember that, or I think I do. I'm not sure because I've heard Mom tell that story so often I may only think I remember. Once when I heard Mom tell that story, I learned something very important to me. I learned that little boys seldom grow up.

If Bev and I are at a party or a gathering, we usually go our separate ways talking to many friends and acquaintances. But every so often we find ourselves together, just for a moment. She may put her arm around me, or I may take her hand. Sometimes it's just our eyes meeting across the room.

Mom's story also helps me understand why it's important for me to pray. At meals, at church, or just casually anytime for a few seconds when I'm doing something else, I need to pray. I need to check in and see that God and others are still there, that I'm loved and needed.

AGING

Children
Play   Matthew 17:1-8
Transfiguration   Mark 9:2-8
Transformation   Luke 9:28-36
Trust   2 Corinthians 4:16-18

A

Sermon
Seasonings

9

Bev and I were staying at Redeemer College in Hamilton, just before the Christian Festival. It was a beautiful day, and I was sitting on a chair out on the lawn reading.

Along the sidewalk came a girl on a tricycle, about six years old was my guess. We smiled at each other.

Then she stopped, gave me a most intense look, and asked, "Are you old?" I'm usually quite quick off the lip, but the child's question stopped me cold. She waited. Maybe she knew she had asked a most profound question. And eventually I responded, "Yes. Yes, I am."

Then she said, "Will you play with me?"

Were the two questions connected in her mind? They were in mine. They said to me, "If you are old, I will trust you." For her, none of the bad jokes they throw at people on their birthdays, just a statement of trust. "Will you play with me?" And I wanted so much to do just that, to hear more from this three-wheeled philosopher, to learn from her wisdom and to delight in the joy of her life. But we live in a real world, my little friend and I. So I had to say, "I would really like to play with you, but first you need to go and talk to your mom or your dad, and if one of them comes here and tells me it's OK, then we can play."

"My dad doesn't live with me anymore," she said very soberly. "I'll ask my mom."

She didn't return. Perhaps she didn't need to. She had left her gift with me. She had given me a tiny transfiguration moment.

She had transfigured me from a man, angry at his age with its limitations and necessities, to a man delighting in his age and in the candid, open and affirming trust of a child.

Yes, little girl. I am old. And yes! Yes, I would like to come and play with you.

AGING

Men
Seniors
Wisdom   James 1:2-11
Women   2 Corinthians 4:16-18

Some women recently have dusted off the word "crone" to denote a wise, older woman who knows what came before and what it cost and can perhaps see more clearly what may come after and what that will cost. Perhaps the word "sage" might do for men.

It is customary at birthday parties around here for the major entertainment to be stories and skits and song parodies about how "old" the person has become. I'm an enthusiastic participant in those exercises. But I'm beginning to object. Yes, I've lost some skills and abilities with the years, but my perception of human spiritual values is far stronger and keener now than it has ever been.

Of course, there are seniors who spend their lives mindlessly filling up the time with bingo and pointless recreation. But most of us have in our bones, bellies and brains a heritage of wisdom. We can see more clearly sometimes, where things are going. That wisdom is a birthright of our children and grandchildren, who have so much information and so little wisdom. Somehow we need to find a way to share that long view with them.

AIDS

Outcasts
Prejudice
Smokers   Luke 17:12ff
Social lepers   2 Samuel 5:6, 8

Leprosy is no longer a medical problem in North America, but the leper syndrome certainly is. We have a variety of "lepers" – people with AIDS, those who are illiterate, various minority groups, folk with some kinds of handicaps, the list could go on. I have a friend who says she and other smokers are treated like "social lepers."

ANDERSON, MARION

Achievement
Courage
Faith
Heritage   Philippians 4:10-13

The world-famous contralto, Marion Anderson, was near retire-ment, when she came to sing in our town. There were times her voice couldn't do what her training demanded. But when she sang "He's Got the Whole World in His Hands" I knew somehow she was sharing her own story of faith and courage. Her voice had the passion of poverty from which she sprang.

Later, when I interviewed her for radio, I saw her hands.

They were the muscled hands of a charwoman.

ASSUMPTIONS

Hearing
Liberation
Preconception
Sexism   John 4:16-18

Every once in awhile I get caught with my assumptions showing.

Everyone knows that the Samaritan woman was a loose-living strumpet who bounced casually from one husband to another. And when she had that conversation with Jesus at the well, she was shacking up with some guy she wasn't married to.

Right.

Except John doesn't say that. I began to squirm when that little fact was called to my attention. If the Bible doesn't say it, how come I "know" it? Yes, Jesus mentions the fact that she's had five hus-bands, but he doesn't call her a "tramp." She is surprised that Jesus knows this about her, but she doesn't seem to feel particularly guilty about it.

Jesus doesn't say she was "divorced" five times. She could just as easily have been widowed five times, and the reason she isn't married to the man she's living with is because she's trapped in the levirate marriage custom and she's stuck with a brother-in-law who won't do his duty. Yes, and that could cause her to be ostracized from the folk in the village, but it's not her fault.

I'm no biblical scholar so I can't really argue the point one way or another. What bugs me is the assumptions I've made – the assumptions I've heard from dozens of pulpits and in many Bible studies – assumptions that are rooted in the virulent sexism of my own mind and of popular culture.

Riding in the car yesterday, listening to an old Simon and Garfunkel tape, I heard the words from their song, *The Boxer*: "...a man hears what he wants to hear, and disregards the rest."

Exactly. But why did I want to hear it that way in the first place?

Awareness comes so slowly, tiny scrap by tidbit, as I wander in the wilderness of my own assumptions, wondering if, before I die, I'll glimpse the promised land of liberation.

ATTENDANCE

Authenticity
Mass Media
Membership
Novelty Luke 15:11ff
Story   1 Corinthians 13:1

Words like "imagination" and "originality" sometimes raise the specter of gimmicky church services that seemed so much the vogue in the '80s and early '70s. Some clergy felt they had to do something new and different every week, something novel – a surprise a Sunday.

That gets us into the same kind of trap television has fallen into, the novelty of each event needing to be just a little more splashy than the one that went before. It's self-defeating.

For the most part, churches have been wiser than commercial media, refusing to offer novelty for its own sake. These media, especially TV, have wasted themselves in excesses, going from specials to super-specials to extra super-specials, until the superlatives and the events they describe have lost their currency with a jaded population. Besides, there's no way the churches can compete with the mass media in producing novelty.

They do have something more durable to offer. That may be one of the reasons people are gradually drifting back into churches. Perhaps they are looking for something that has quality and content. Maybe they are searching for something genuine.

It may be the prodigal instinct. The strange land offered no real substance, no real relationships, no ultimate meaning. Now they are coming home to be accepted and loved, looking for something to believe in.

This is both an opportunity and a terrible danger. Reacting against the excess of novelty in past years, we can easily fall back into the trap of mindless monotony. The church must tell the old, old story, but that story must grow in the living of people or it dies. It must be a story that involves congregations in the telling, a story with life, vitality and mystery.

ATTITUDE
Point of View
Risk   Matthew 14:22-33

Bruce Hatfield chuckled through the whole telling. A city bus had been hit by another vehicle near his house. The driver had been knocked from his seat and the bus had gone careening down the street finally stopping on a neighbor's lawn.

Bruce, a physician, ran over to see if he could help.

No one was seriously injured, but said Bruce, "a young woman came off the bus, her face absolutely ashen, her hands trembling. She had a little guy in tow, about five years old, who said, "Gee, Mom, that was a great ride. Can we do it again?'"

AUTHENTICITY
Apostle Peter
Guileless Devotion
Humility   John 1:43-51

He was big and bony and he had spent his lifetime fishing the Galilee. His name wasn't Peter, but I can't help but think of him as a kind of reincarnation of the big, bony Peter who fished the same waters two thousand years ago.

So I'll call him Peter. Besides, I can't remember his real name.

He had come from Czechoslovakia to Israel as a boy, and joined the kibbutz Ein Gev. Somewhere along the way he became interested in archeology, and became the area's most respected amateur archeologist. Among his interests – the New Testament accounts of fishing the Galilee.

A few years ago, when the lake was unusually low, he walked all the way around the lake looking at the newly exposed shoreline. Not far from Ein Gev, he found the remains of a first-century fishing boat, the kind that Peter might have used. Public imagination being what it was, the boat has been named, St. Peter's boat, though of course there is no way of knowing who may have owned it or used it.

I was at Ein Gev with a group doing biblical studies, and "Peter" was asked to come and show his slides and talk about what he knew of New Testament fishing practices. It was a fascinating talk, but what fascinated me more was his wonderful incompetence in handling his slide projector, his screen and some of the artifacts. He got slides in upside down, in the wrong order, the projector was unfocused, etc. etc. In his talk he kept tripping on his words and forgetting his place.

But the man was utterly genuine. "Peter" simply was what he was. No more, no less. I don't think he could have told a lie if he had tried and he certainly didn't know how to boast about his accomplishments and his knowledge, though they were considerable. He had obviously memorized all four gospels (he was a devout Jew), and made wonderful connections between that and life on the Galilee today. "Peter" could hardly tie his shoes and sometimes said the dumbest things. But he was clearly a genius.

I couldn't help seeing Peter, the friend of Jesus. A man of astounding insight and utter stupidity. He would trip on the carpet but he could recognize the face of God. Not an ounce of guile in his being. A man capable of total devotion.

But he probably couldn't hold a steady job in any business, nor would he last a year in any pulpit.

BAPTISM

Confirmation	
Initiation	Matthew 3:13-17
Peace	Mark 1:9-11

I was baptized twice last summer.

The first time was in the Sea of Galilee. It was our first night beside that historic lake, and because it was hot and because I was utterly thrilled by the sheer idea of being there, I couldn't wait to get to that water, half expecting to be able to walk on it.

Something better happened. I stood there, up to my neck in water, and looked around and imagined Jesus and Peter and Mary of Magdala and all the world-changing events that happened around and on that lake. And I felt a profound sense of awe and joy that I had received that heritage. And so I soaked in the warm waters and soaked in the history of the hills of Galilee. And I came out an hour later feeling, yes, baptized.

A week later we were up near Dan, and there in that source of the Jordan, where the water is still clean and cold, I filled some bottles of that "holy" water to bring home for the baptism of an expected grandchild.

Standing up to my knees in the rushing water, I wanted to be baptized again. I was baptized when I was just over 20, but I knew so little then, had lived so little. It didn't mean that much then, but it would mean so much now. Why not do it now, again?

It was not for want of clergy. There were at least a dozen ordained Roman Catholic priests in my group, but I knew full well none of them could, or should, baptize me there and then.

So I cupped some water in my hands and poured the Jordan over my head and face, and said a small prayer of gratitude, and felt a deep and fundamental peace.

Perhaps it wasn't baptism. Perhaps it was a confirmation of the half-understood words I uttered 35 years ago. Perhaps it was fulfillment of a promise made by God to me when Dave Stone poured that water on my head.

That's interesting. Baptism is just once. The confirmation, the fulfillment happens over and over and over. God's gift is limitless.

BAPTISM

Citizenship
Family
Grandchildren
Heritage
Security   Ephesians 2:19-22

Our grandson Jake was baptized a few weeks ago. Jake went through the whole process with an expression of detached amusement on his face. I'm sure he was convinced the process was primarily for the benefit of his parents and grandparents, and he was quite right. We baptize our babies because it helps us understand a little of what family and church and faith is. For the moment, he needs no explanations. Jake knows. He feels it in the warmth of his family, in the security of the love that surrounds him, even in the asinine antics of his granddad trying to make him laugh.

Jake was baptized in water from the Jordan which I brought with me when I went there on sabbatical a year and a half ago, and with that symbol comes all the rich heritage of struggle and faith of his Judeo-Christian forebears. He was baptized into a church by his uncle (Brian Jackson), surrounded by two parents, four grandparents, numerous relatives and members of a church, a commonwealth of faith, in which his parents are active. Now – that is one lucky child. Now – that is a child with a problem.

Jake is both blessed and cursed, because that same doting family and those same kind friends will lead him from his primitive infant wisdom into adult knowledge – adult apostasy. Whether we choose to or not, we will lead him and mislead him.

Jake will imitate us. Lucky kid. Poor kid.

Jake will learn about God from us. Lucky kid. Poor kid.
Jake has his citizenship in the family – the commonwealth we have created. Lucky kid. Poor kid.

But Jake, like every child, has God on his side. If somehow, in his baptism and in our lives we can show him that, he'll be OK.

BAPTISM
Children
Confession of Faith   Matthew 16:15, 27:54
Jesus   Mark 8:27-29, 15:39
Response   Luke 9:18-20

When you've seen one baptism, you've seen 'em all.

Well, not quite. This was when Bev (my wife) was minister at the Westbank Church. It was a baptism of two young children in a family, one about three and the other about five. Bev explained that not only had she met with the parents to explain the meaning of baptism, she had met with the two children separately. And all four of them were going to make a personal statement of faith.

First the parents. Their statements obviously reflected the words and phrases they had heard and read. That was OK. They seemed eager to learn and grow.

Then the eldest of the two children said, "I like Jesus because he's nice." And the youngest child held up a picture he had colored. We weren't sure what it was, but Bev made it quite clear that she appreciated all four statements and valued them equally.

The four members of that family, in effect, responded to Jesus' question: "Who do you say that I am?" And in the sermon Bev, in effect, offered her response.

I arranged those five statements in my head in terms of relative merit beginning with the colored picture, all the way through Bev's sermon. And I'd no sooner done that than I recognized the heresy in that.

There are no adequate responses to that question. But by the same token, there are no inadequate responses either. There's no grading system – no prize for the "right" answer. "Jesus is nice," differs only in sophistication, but not in correctness or authenticity from Bev's sermon.

BELIEF

Christology
Faith
Intellectualism   Romans 10:6-13
Presence   Deuteronomy 30:11-14

Right at the moment, there is a marmot trying to take up residence under our back porch. It's a brown, furry rodent of indeterminate sex (at least I couldn't determine it) about the size of a small cat. I like marmots normally, out in the hills where you usually see them sitting upright near their burrows. But this one is sitting upright on my back stoop, and from the width of his girth I think he may be a she – a mama in waiting and I really don't want my porch to be a marmot maternity ward.

Sitting on the back porch is a wire grid, some staples and a hammer. As soon as that marmot leaves to get some lunch, I nail up another hole, and as soon as the marmot comes back from lunch he/she finds yet another hole and proceeds to do whatever it is that marmots do under porches.

All of which is kind of a ham-handed metaphor of my Christology. Just when I have read another book by Burton Mack or Marcus Borg and patched up the holes in my latest, neatest theory, the resurrected, historical Jesus slips right back in again. A few years ago I spent several hours in a car with Matthew Fox and found myself quite excited about his Cosmic Christ, but, well, I backslid.

It would be such a relief, wouldn't it, to have a nice simple answer for the Christ question? Sometimes I long for the simplicity of belief I see in some friends for whom Jesus is a real and palpable presence and maybe that's why my real Christology, (what I actually think as opposed to what I think I should think) is pretty orthodox. I'm not all that far from a friend who will begin a statement with, "I was talking to Jesus this morning...." I have a really hard time grasping the reality of a cosmic consciousness or a spiritual energy field.

Is ignorance bliss? If it's true that what you don't know can hurt you, it may also be true that what you do know can also hurt you. I know too many theories, and all of them are as full of holes as my back porch.

And that rodent redeemer keeps finding a way to get back in. Maybe I should stop patching and (like Paul) get excited by what I've experienced.

BIBLE STUDY
Bible, Interpretation of
Community
Hearing
Lectionary
Prophecy   Luke 2:41-45

I've talked to numbers of clergy who begin their sermon preparation in this way. Darryl Auten of Salmon Arm, BC, has three lectionary study groups early each week. There's a breakfast meeting for people who have jobs to go to, a noon-hour session for   seniors, and another in the evening.

Clergy who have organized such lectionary study groups don't see it as a means of gathering anecdotes to add spice to the sermon, although those do come along occasionally.

Many of the stories told in a study group cannot be shared publicly. In fact, it really isn't a means of gathering sermon material at all. It doesn't cut down on sermon preparation time or make the process any easier. It does make it richer.

These clergy see the process as a way of entering into the lives of those with whom they will share the preaching experience. God's covenant is with the community. God's word comes to the community. And unless we wrestle with the scripture in community, we are not likely to hear the Gospel. If we cannot hear the Gospel, how can we preach it?

There are added benefits. It does wonders for the preacher to notice people listening intently and intelligently. Those who were at the lectionary Bible study group are anxious and interested to hear a reflection based on the wrestling they did. Preachers try harder because they know somebody is actually listening.

There's more. When the hard prophetic things must be said, there are at least a few people from the congregation who have helped the preacher be prophetic in a way that will be heard rather than simply resented. When the prophecy is preached, these people are more likely to hear. And they will help their friends in the congregation hear.

BIBLE, INTERPRETATION OF
Disagreement
Faith
Fundamentalism
Liberalism   2 Timothy 3:16

In the church, we have lost the Bible, the richest source of our Christian mythology. The right wing has embalmed the biblical story in its desperate attempt to keep it unchanging and totally dependable. The left wing of the church has dissected the scriptural myth, taken it out of the hands of the priests and given it to the scholars. Bishops have rescued the Bible from fundamentalism, but not given it to the people. Scholars gratuitously offer information on what Jesus certainly said or certainly did not say, distracting us from the mythological truth injected by writers and editors and copyists to whom the spirit also whispered.

And nowhere have we heard the clear, unequivocal statement – it's OK to disagree with the Bible. Hear the song that gives you life. Let others hear their song which may not be your song. Lay the rest gently aside for someone else to sing.

BREAD

Basics
Comfort
Food

Matthew 6:11
Luke 11:3
John 6

"When you are out of peanut butter, you are out of food."

That is a proposition I have defended passionately, and unsuccessfully, since as far back as I can remember. When I am feeling down, when I've been sick, when I just want a snack, when I'm having lunch by myself, I'll have a peanut butter and jam sandwich on whole-wheat bread.

"It's a complete meal," I argue. "The peanuts and the whole wheat have all those amino acids being amiable and providing protein. And the fruit in the jam provides me with all I need in terms of fruit and veggies."

If only my family would argue with me, I could prove to them how right I am. But all I get are those "there goes Dad again" indulgent looks as they walk off to be busy with something else.

I've heard people use the phrase "comfort food," and I guess that's what a peanut butter and jam sandwich is to me. If I had to survive the rest of my life on one thing, that would be it.

In English, the word "bread," in some contexts, is synonymous with food. In many East Asian dialects, the word for "rice" and the word for "food" are the same. In some Melanesian languages, the same applies to yams. It's whatever is the bottom line. It's the basic thing you need to stay alive. For a newborn child, it would be mother's milk.

But all those words – bread, rice, yams, milk – can also refer to the emotional and spiritual basics that keep us alive. There are a few people without whose love I would find it hard, perhaps impossible, to live. And without a faith that gets fed and watered regularly, I'd dry up and blow away.

Bread is the biblical metaphor, simply because that was the staple, basic, bottom-line food of Jesus' time. If Jesus had been Melanesian, it would have been yams.

As for me, when my time comes to stand before the firing squad, and the chaplain comes to give me my last communion, I would like the "bread" to be a peanut butter and jam sandwich. And the wine? Well, how about a good, dry Chianti.

Chianti normally gives me a terrible headache, but hey! Life is short!

Ministry
Patience
Trust   Hebrews 11:8
Vocation   Genesis 12:1-8

Sermon
Seasonings

21

As far back as I can remember, people were asking me, "What are you going to be when you grow up?"

As a kid, I probably had some ideas about being a cowboy or a pilot, or something. I can't remember. I can't ever remember wanting to be anything in particular, nor for that matter can I remember wanting to grow up.

Many years later, when I was about 45, they rephrased the question. "What are your career objectives?"

I didn't know the answer then, and I don't know it now. What I do know is that through most of my adult life both Bev and I have felt a gentle hand in the small of the back gently pushing us to do things we'd never thought of on our own.

Just after we were married, I found myself flailing about, not wanting to do my work at a small radio station in Trail, BC. I was a "jock" running one of the very first open-line shows in Canada – a bit of history my teenage daughters find hard to believe.

We pushed at all sorts of doors looking for a way into something more meaningful. They slammed shut in our faces. Finally, we decided just to hunker down and stay where we were. There didn't seem to be any other option.

We'd no sooner done that, than a door we'd never dreamed of swung open. Missionary work in the Philippines, where we spent five fantastic years.

The pattern repeated itself when we moved to New York, then when we went to Calgary, and again coming to the Okanagan. Each time we've banged at doors that wouldn't open. As soon as we gave up and decided to stay put, something turned up that wasn't quite what we were thinking of, but exactly what we needed.

CHARISMATIC

Evangelical
Holy Spirit
Preconceived Ideas
Tongues   Acts 2

There I was in a meeting of the Full Gospel Businessmen. I went because it was easier than fending off Bert's enthusiasm. Bert insisted I "come and see."

So I came. I saw. I left.

Mostly I was amazed how those guys could stand with their hands up for ten minutes at a stretch. Maybe the "infilling of the spirit" helped them. It didn't help me. My hands went dead after two minutes.

Watching a wealthy middle-aged car dealer in a three-piece suit, hands up in the air, talking what seemed to me to be gibberish had me wondering if I was in the middle of a Monty Python movie. Bert didn't call it gibberish, of course. He called it the Holy Spirit.

I don't argue with Bert. He has the second chapter of the book of Acts on his side. When you think of it, a car dealer in a three piece suit is no stranger than an oversized fisherman nicknamed "Rocky" speaking gibberish. Or tongues. As the book of Acts tells it, the folk standing around thought Peter and his crowd were a bit strange too. "Stoned," they said. Or the first century equivalent thereof.

CHARISMATIC

Community
Holy Spirit
Tongues   Philippians 1:27-30, 2:2

I was at a meeting of a charismatic group in Lethbridge.

The very first thing that struck me . . . "what a sense of community." Their common story was their discovery of the "spirit" and to that story they added others as they prayed for guidance in a host of small and large problems, from the need for a new job to support for an alcoholic husband. The story of the "infilling of the spirit" was most important to the community because it identified them. They were active, civic-minded citizens all of them, but they came away from that to this meeting to be a community, a people.

Their uniqueness drew them together, and they were pushed together by the rest of society and the church which often sees charismatics as a bit "kooky."

CHILDREN

Jesus and children
Ministry of children
Respect
Worth

Matthew 19:13-15, 18:1-7
Mark 10:13-16, 9:36-42
Luke 18:16, 9:47-48

I was looking at a very old photo album. The adults and the children stood stiffly in rows.

It was interesting. The children didn't look like children. They looked like small adults. Then I remembered somebody observing that it's only been in recent years that we've had such a thing as children's clothes. Before that, we simply had small versions of adult clothes.

Children in biblical times had little value. Any value they had lay in what they might become. A boy child would become a man, and men of course ran the world. A girl child would become a woman who could bear children. But in and of themselves, children were not valued except as potential adults.

All of which has me shaking my head about Jesus. He picked up a child. I mean picked it right up in his arms and said, "If you really want to know what it's all about, learn from this child." The people around him must have thought he'd fallen out of his tree. Grown men, respected rabbis, simply didn't do things like that. But Jesus clearly liked children.

And Jesus respected children, which is a different thing altogether. Some people like children they way they like pets. Jesus was convinced that children had a wisdom most adults have lost, and that quite literally, our salvation depends on learning how to receive the ministry of children.

CHILDREN'S STORIES IN CHURCH

Creativity
Imagination
Originality   1 Corinthians 3:1-2
Sermons   Hebrews 5:12 – 6:3

Like most pew-sitters, I've often enjoyed the children's sermon more than the one intended for adults. That says something about the preacher and about me. The children's sermon may have been the only point at which I made a bit of effort, where I participated by imagining along with the preacher and the kids. On the other hand, it may also mean that the kids' sermon was the only place where the preacher showed a bit of imagination, a bit of originality in style, and told a story.

CHRISTMAS

Community
Concerts
Inclusiveness   Luke 2:15-18
Participation   1 Peter 2:9-10

The Christmas concert at our school in Horndean was always the most important event of the whole year. Dad was the school teacher and he organized everything. For weeks, our parents would be having secret meetings so the kids couldn't hear. It was all we could do to bear the suspense.

The Christmas concert was a ritual. Everyone in the community was there, and everyone was involved. All the kids in the school sang in the choir, and each one was also in a play or sang or recited. It didn't matter how well or how badly you did, everyone always clapped.

The main feature was the pageant, when Mary and Joseph and the baby Jesus, the kings and the shepherds, resplendent in their towels and bathrobes, would act out the ancient story while an older child read from the Bible. The pageant always concluded with "Stille Nacht, Heilige Nacht." Then came the presents. A red net bag of goodies and a small gift from Santa.

It was always the same and always different. Everybody had a stake in what happened.

We were saying to ourselves, "This is us! We are a community! We are a people!"

CHRISTMAS

Caring
Community
Concerts
Empathy
Enthusiasm
Participation   Matthew 2:1-15

They packed the hall on Sunday night. Every chair we had was set up, and people stood around the edges. It was a celebration of Christmas and a celebration of community.

The Elementary School choir got us off to a happy start with a set of rollicking songs.

Tanya Jones blushed and Chris Warrington boomed their way through solo parts. And by the time they were finished we all knew exactly why we had come.

Then the Grade Three choir lisped their way through a clutch of carols, and the Junior Choir from the church bounced us through a couple of snappy Christmas hymns.

Diane Friesen directed with everything she was, from her toe nails to her hair follicles. It showed in her shoulders, in her hips and the sway of her head. I kept wishing I could see her face. The kids could, and her enthusiasm reflected in their eyes.

There were no spectators. They were our kids, our family, our friends, our neighbors. And even though we weren't on stage, emotionally at least, we were participants.

We felt even worse than Tony did when his music fell off the piano and he had to start all over again. And when the Grade Three choir got a bit mixed up in their story of Silent Night we struggled as hard as they to get the thing together again.

That's what community means. Feeling the pain when things go wrong, and shouting together when things go right. And celebrating both.

There wasn't a thing in that program that was good enough for television. In fact, if you squeezed it through the wires and transistors of a television transmission, all the juice would have been lost and you'd have had nothing but a badly done amateur hour.

Come to think of it though, the evening was really much too good for television. We'd been brought together by the love that's there in the middle of Christmas. And though we came from different religious traditions, or none at all, we were all there because we cared about somebody else; somebody who was playing or singing or reading.

And caring about somebody else is somewhere near the heart of Christmas.

CHRISTMAS

Family
Festival
Liturgy
Rituals   Matthew 2
Santa   Luke 2

Christmas at our house when I was a child was a ritual. The night before we would set out plates on the table with our names on them.

Dad would always get up first Christmas morning, making a terrible noise banging on the furnace to get the clinkers out.

Then we'd always gather and sing "Silent Night," and everyone would eat a Japanese orange. Then the presents!

Even after we were all adults, we tried to keep the ritual intact. On one occasion, when we were all going to be together Christmas eve but not Christmas day, we put our pajamas on, went to bed for 18 minutes, then got up and "had Christmas," complete with the banging of the furnace. It was important to do that, even though we laughed at ourselves.

We have festivals because we cannot live without them. Now I have a family of my own. We've developed a ritual of our own, springing out of the traditions brought together by Bev and myself and spiced with the imaginations of our children.

We have stockings, not plates. But we all gather in our bedroom, walk to the tree together singing "Silent Night," eat an orange and then open our gifts. And for a little while at least, we all believe in Santa.

CHRISTMAS
Danger
Humility
Pain   Luke 2:6
Suffering   Matthew 2:7-8, 16-18, 13-14

I bumped my head in Bethlehem.

The door to the Church of the Holy Nativity is only about four feet high. We were warned by our guide, but of course, I forgot – and soft head against hard rock doesn't produce a pleasant sensation.

Tradition has it that the low door was installed so that we would stoop when we entered the sanctuary, and remember to bow in the presence of the infant Jesus. Humility is the proper attitude with which to approach the Savior.

In reality, the low door was put in because people were shorter in those days, and because they wanted to keep thoughtless people from riding right into church on their horses. But I bumped my head and it reminded me, not to bow, but to remember that Jesus' birth, as well as his death, involved pain and danger.

The awareness of pain didn't penetrate until I knelt at the traditional site of the manger (and probably the actual site) beside a woman from our group who had been through considerable pain in her life. She was a mother of four. She was weeping as she prayed, and I remembered reflecting on how Mary must have felt, alone, afraid, with no mother or midwife to see her through the pain and fear of birth.

And the danger part came home when I looked out from Bethlehem and saw Jerusalem on the horizon. Nowadays, Bethlehem is virtually a suburb of Jerusalem. In Jesus' day, it was six miles away. That's only an hour and a half of walking – much less on a good horse. And I couldn't help but wonder if the Magi had seen through Herod's charade and rushed to warn Joseph and Mary. The whole thing – the visit of the Magi, the flight to Egypt, the slaughter of the children of Bethlehem – could have happened in a few hours.

Hard stone on a soft head can be a learning experience. Sometimes it can be God trying to get in to remind me not to be too romantic about Christmas.

CHRISTMAS

Gifts
Humor
Joke   Isaiah 9:2-7, 52:7-10
Messiah   Micah 5:2-4
Unexpected   Luke 2

It's a marvelous, wonderful, wise, loving, practical joke.

Christmas! The nativity.

There's God, down through the centuries, listening to the prophecies about the Messiah.

Some of them were wonderful and beautiful and spoke the mind of God.

Others thundered away about the Conqueror, the one who'd come in on a white horse, with sword and shield, a leader that would be better and tougher than King David.

So God gave them the gift they so badly needed. But not the gift they expected.

It was King David II they wanted. It was a tiny baby they got. What a hoot!

They wanted power. So God gave them the power of weakness. They wanted a conqueror. So God gave them love that conquers all.

That must have been good for a heavenly chuckle or perhaps even a belly laugh, if a belly laugh is possible for a God who is spirit.

It was not the laughter of derision. It was the laughter of a loving, gentle parent waking up long before the kids on Christmas morning, waking up in anticipation of the face of the child when that special gift is opened, the child who receives so much more than it ever dared ask for in the letter to Santa.

And the laughter of God is the laughter of a pleased-as-punch parent who receives the Christmas thank-you hug of a delighted child.

The joke comes back every year.

CHRISTMAS

Gifts
Peacekeeper
Toys
War
War toys   Matthew 2:16-18
Violence   Luke 2

'Twas the night before Christmas
When all through the house,
Nothing was stirring,
Especially my spouse.

My spouse was zonked out
After spending the night,
Wrapping the robot
With its laser light.

We'd had a big supper
Where we both dropped our diet,
Then an hour in church
Telling Junior, "Be quiet!"

The robot was big,
It had batteries included.
All over its frame
Deadly weapons extruded.

Wrapping was hard,
Guns poked through the paper,
And my spouse cut a hand,
On the robot's steel rapier.

So my spouse had a scotch,
Then a hot rum or two,
And the robot got wrapped
Though a ray gun stuck through.

The robot, we thought
Was a most fitting gift...
A good Christmas trifle
To give Junior a lift.

Junior's asleep now.
The child's tired right out.
He threw a huge tantrum,
We're not sure what about.

A robot's the right gift
To give to our sleeper
to remind him of Jesus.
It's called the "Peacekeeper."

CHRISTMAS

Chosen
Gifts
Giving   James 1:17
Love   Luke 2:19

It was a hot and sticky summer day on the prairies. If we stood in the sunshine we got burned. If we stood in the shade we got bitten by mosquitoes.

But we were singing Christmas carols, even "In the bleak midwinter..."

It was a Lutheran family camp and Bev and I were leading them through the church year in five days. Advent, Christmas, Lent, Easter and Pentecost. Five seasons in five days. Christmas was the big hit. Everybody knew what that was about, including the children, and when we announced that "Today is Christmas Day," there was a big cheer. Visions of "dividing the spoils" and Christmas dinner pig-outs danced through a few heads.

Except that we were twenty miles from the nearest store and we said right at the beginning, "What we do – we will do with what we find here at the camp."

So we spent the day getting ready for our Christmas celebration that evening. It would include the giving of gifts, but we needed to talk about what gifts were really about. How do you know what to give somebody until you know what somebody really wants? So members of the various families talked to each other and in various ways asked the questions, "What gift can I give you this Christmas?"

No trips to Sears were possible. Money was not a factor because there was nothing to be bought. After some kidding around and embarrassed first starts, people got to talking to each other. And when the gifts were given that evening, there were twigs and rocks and flowers and feathers. But each gift was carefully, thoughtfully chosen and each came with an expression of love and care, which was of course the real gift.

One small child brought the remains of a robin's egg to her mother and gave it along with a sweaty hug. And the mother gave her daughter a small wild rosebud and a kiss. No words were possible or necessary.

That night under the starlight, like Mary, all of us "kept those things and pondered them" in our hearts.

CHURCH CONFERENCES
Justice
Relevance
Seeds   Matthew 13:18-20, 31-32
Social Conscience   Luke 8:4-8, 13:18-19
Song   Mark 4:1-9

Like six hundred other people of good intentions and high motivation, I will soon attend a meeting of the BC Conference of the United Church. I go because I am noble of heart, because I am utterly dedicated to the work of my church, and because I am such a fine, generous (and humble) person.

I also go because a bunch of fun people come to the conference and we get together around the coffee urn and tell each other the latest jokes and swap the latest gossip. And if I spend enough time around the coffee urn and as little time as possible on "the floor," I know my time is well spent.

But there are times. When we begin debating an amendment to an amendment "fine-tuning" the language of a motion which is to be sent to the government of Canada expressing our "concern" about Nicaragua or South Africa or whatever, knowing full well that the most we can expect by way of governmental response is a yawn, then I wonder.

600 of us! If we spend five minutes at it, that's 50 people hours!

And yet we must do this. We should do this. We are a thin, squeaky voice crying in the wilderness. We squawk and fuss in all seriousness, while at the same time laughing a little at ourselves; at the ludicrousness of it all; at the futility of singing the Lord's song in this insane land.

We must laugh while we do this, or we will go mad. If we delude ourselves with a sense of relevance or importance, we will be fools in the worst sense of the word. If we know how silly we look to the rest of the world, and how God must be smiling at our feeble flailing about, yet sing our song and tell our story with our whole being, then we will be fools in the godly sense of the word.

We will be fools who plant tiny seeds in God's garden; fools who know very well that most of the seeds will die under wheels of profit or shrivel in the acid rain of cynicism.

But somewhere, a seed will grow again and bloom. Somewhere. Sometime.

CLERGY

Evangelism	
Humor	
Honesty	Matthew 10:19-20
Outreach	Mark 13:11
Vocation	Luke 8:8-12, 12:49-51
Work	John 15:18

Every clergy person I've ever talked with will tell of the temptation to lie when conversing with a stranger and the question, "So what sort of work are you in?" comes up.

Not being of the ordained persuasion, but nonetheless in a full-time Christian vocation, I can duck the question. "I'm a writer," doesn't bring the conversation to a grinding thud the way, "Clergy" sometimes does. At least until they ask what kinds of things I write.

There is good news. Part of the good news is that God has gifted most clergy with a healthy sense of humor which is a cooling balm for such social nettles. Clergy (and their spouses) with a commitment to sanity will gather with other clergy to do a bit of creative bellyaching and some healthy laughing at the ludicrousness of it all.

Those clergy who think it might help, or who simply want to get it off their chest, will preach a sermon based on Galatians that might be titled, "Let's get real about the Rev." Others will do whatever is necessary to develop a strong and vital spirituality, will focus on their sense of call, and will know they are living one of the most difficult and most life-giving vocations. "If we live by the Spirit, let us also be guided by the Spirit."

As for me, I'm going to do a short article titled, "How to grow eggplant for fun and profit," just so I can tell people that's what I write.

CLERGY

Attitudes toward clergy	Matthew 10:19-20	Luke 8:8-12, 12:49-51
Stereotypes	Mark 13:11	John 15:18

With a few exceptions, clergy dread wedding and funeral receptions. They dislike them because they feel isolated and lonely, and the folks who talk to them inevitably make some damn fool comment based on images of clergy portrayed in old movies or third-rate romance novels. It's no wonder some clergy go overboard (sometimes inappropriately) to prove they are really just "one of the folks."

It's hardest when there are gatherings of relatives. Aunts, uncles and cousins try to reconcile a saccharine image of "a reverend" with the reality of the you they have known over the years. "Jack was always in trouble. He worried his parents sick. And now he's a minister?"

It's extra hard for female ministers, particularly young, good looking female ministers, who have to battle old images of sexless tea-sipping parsons.

I have no idea what to do about this. I do know that many clergy find it helpful, once in awhile, to get together with other clergy and just talk about what it is like to be clergy and to bellyache about us laypeople.

CLERGY

Feedback		
Rejoinders	Matthew 10:19-20	Luke 8:8-12, 12:49-51
Sermons	Mark 13:11	John 15:18

When clergy gather, they sometimes talk about things nobody else talks about.

One of those conversations took place at PCTC. (Prairie Christian Training Center) in Fort Qu'Appelle, Sask. Audrey Kaldestad was the ring leader. She and Barb Tedrick were comparing favorite comments from parishioners as they shake hands at the door on

Sunday morning. Anyway, Barb and Audrey started a list, to which we hope you and others will add.

"I just don't know where you come up with all that stuff," to which the appropriate reply would be, "Especially without a book allowance." "Good sermon! What book did you use?" is a kind of backhanded compliment. The rejoinder? "I don't use books. God speaks directly to me."

"Well done. I'm sure you made a point," is another complimentary insult. "Yes I did. But I didn't expect you to get it."

"Good morning. Why didn't you turn down the thermostat?" After all, the clergy are in charge of everything. "Where is it?" might be some helpful reality training.

"Nice day. Glad to be able to go to the beach now." "Me too!"

"Welcome back. So you've been on study leave. Did you learn anything?" "I have two hours free on Tuesday afternoon. Please come by and I'll tell you about it."

Then there's that intergenerational Sunday when all the kids are there for the whole service, and someone asks, "Where were all the Sunday school teachers?" Again, some reality therapy. "It was their annual day off."

I shared with Audrey and Barb my frustration at having poured heart and soul into the content of a sermon and then being confronted at the church door with, "I loved your voice. I could listen to you all day." If I'd had the nerve, I'd have yelled in my best Lorne Greene pear-shaped tones, "I wasn't singing!"

Perhaps the all-time favorite Sunday morning compliment was one which Audrey and cohorts thought was a bit sexist, till I told them that I, as a 55ish, 6 foot male of the species had also received this *bon mot*.

"That was lovely, dear."

CLERGY, FEMALE
Normalcy
Stereotypes

Actually, I'm disgustingly normal. It's just that I have a talent for finding myself in slightly abnormal circumstances.

Like being married to a minister. Never having been married to anyone else, it's hard to compare. But it feels normal. In fact, I'd even be prepared to say we're in love. After 39 years!

Even after all this time some of our relatives still haven't got it all straight. We got a long letter asking in terribly polite language, how to address a letter to a couple when she is a "Rev." and he is nothing in particular.

"It's easy," I say. "Just send it to 'Rev. & Mr.' or 'Mr. & Rev.' Whatever you like. How about just 'Bev and Ralph'?"

But when you tell people that, you can almost see their mental computers overloading. Sometimes people shuffle from one foot to another trying to ask me what it's like being married to a lady minister.

"I was married to her long before she was a minister," I usually say. "When she became a minister it didn't seem to make any difference. Same girl."

That doesn't seem to be enough for them, so I usually add, "Lots of guys have their wives preach at them but mine is specially trained." It's slightly sexist but it seems to lower their anxiety a bit.

CLERGY, FEMALE
Assumptions
Identity
Marriage
Relationships   Ephesians 4:13ff

Bev was a shy, skinny grade four school teacher. I was a macho DJ at the local radio station. She and I took an instant dislike to each other. She thought I was conceited. I thought she was dull.

But we hung around the edges of the same gang, and so managed to continue our dislike for several years.

Then her boyfriend went off to the west coast to study and she needed a ride to the hospital for physiotherapy on a bad disk in her back. Call it a mystery or a miracle, but the disk healed and the dislike dissolved into love. We were married the following fall.

Our relationship was very typical. Very normal. I set out to conquer the world and she set out to populate it. That was the way God had ordained things, wasn't it?

It's only looking back that I realize the changes. Gradually, bit by bit, Bev came out of her shell, and gradually, bit by bit, I discovered my humanity. A few of the assumptions about our relationship and her identity began to be challenged. Just a little.

She studied theology on the side, and earned a degree, *magna cum laude*. The significance of that escaped me at the time. Eventually she became an ordained minister, an event that shook me right down to my toe nails.

This wasn't the girl I married. But then, neither was I the boy she married. And suddenly a whole bunch of things about our relationship needed to be rethought – renegotiated – revisioned.

CLERGY, FEMALE

Assumptions
Marriage
Relationships
Sexuality
Virgin birth   Matthew 1:18-24

People who haven't been to church since they dropped out of Sunday school seem to have strange outdated ideas of what it's all about, and they get themselves into the silliest corners. Imagine this at a service club meeting.

"What did you say your name was?" We were standing around trying to recover from an after-lunch speaker.

"Milton, Ralph."

"Don't I know you from somewhere? The name sounds familiar."

"Possibly. More likely you know my wife. She's the minister at one of the churches here in town."

There's a long silence while that sinks in. Then trying to say something, he sputters, "Ah...do you have a family?" He blushes deep red, and I wonder why.

"Yes, we have four children."

The man is obviously surprised. "My God," he mutters. Then clearing his throat, he recovers slightly and says, "I mean, a clergyman having babies...ah...I mean...." The man is completely flustered.

"Relax," I say as kindly as possible. "Clergymen seldom have babies, but clergywomen do, and they do exactly what other women do in order to get them."

There's a pause, then a giggle, finally a laugh.

"Isn't it amazing the assumptions we make when we don't stop to think. Well, anyway, can I buy you a cup of coffee or something? Being married to a minister, you must need something to steady your nerves now and again."

"Amen," I say as we head down the corridor to the coffee shop. "In fact anybody married to anybody needs their nerves steadied now and again."

CLOWNS

Fools for Christ
Humor
Storyteller
Symbols
Vulnerable   1 Corinthians 1:9-10, 18-25

Floyd Shaefer, a Lutheran pastor, understands the concept of "tears dipped in honey. " It's part of his "clown ministry."

At a meeting in Ft. Lauderdale, Florida, Floyd led us through a complete worship service. He didn't speak a word. His story was told in gesture and symbols, and his priestly vestments were the costume of a clown. Deep inside me, I suddenly made a connection between being a clown and being a Christian.

I'm not sure I have the skills to describe what I mean in words, because these ideas can really only be contained in symbols that are much larger than language. But I'll try.

As a clown, I think Pastor Shaefer sees himself as deeply human and essentially comic. A clown is completely vulnerable.

He expects and receives no status, no honor. He is least among the great, the court jester. There is always the real possibility that we may laugh *at* him. But if we look deeply into his sad eyes and see beyond the false nose and the makeup, we will see ourselves and we will laugh *with* him.

We too become vulnerable to the laughter and ridicule of others while we search the crowd for the eyes of someone who will laugh with us.

COMMUNICATION

Dialogue
Listening
Outcome   Matthew 15:21-28, 20:29-34
Personality Differences   Mark 7:24-30, 10:46-52
Understanding   Luke 18:35-43

It brought a flood of memories. In the paper was a write-up about Roy Calvert, a key figure in the Salvation Army. He died last summer. And as I read of his death, I realized I was grateful for what he had taught me.

Roy and I were part of an Alberta Interfaith television production team producing weekly programs on a network of five stations. This was in Calgary two decades ago.

Often we had people coming to our group wanting us to do a program on a particular topic, and some of those people were walking on the edges of any reality I recognized. My inclination was always to get rid of them as quickly as possible and get on with the job.

But Roy would have none of that. He wanted to understand them. Roy would ask questions and listen intently to the response. He would ask and listen until he was satisfied he really understood. It sometimes took hours and we often got impatient. But Roy was genuinely interested in people and wanted to know where they came from.

An amazing thing invariably happened in these conversations between Roy and the assorted "weirdos." After awhile, the diatribe turned into a dialogue. As these folk gradually became aware that Roy was genuinely interested, they would ask him, "What do you think?" and they would listen to his answer. And then a real dialogue began.

COMMUNICATION
Charismatic
Ecumenism
Holy Spirit   Acts 2:4
Tongues   1 Corinthians 12:1-end

About a year ago, I went with two new friends to worship at the Anglican church in Jerusalem's old city. They were two retired nurses working at a convent near Jerusalem, both of them recently from Vancouver near where I live – one of them originally from Jamaica.

The Jamaican woman entered the church first, and the usher immediately showed her to the middle of a large unoccupied section. We followed.

Soon we were surrounded by a huge Nigerian delegation. My Jamaican friend thought it must have been her black skin that had the usher thinking she was part of that group. It was a mistake we enjoyed, because the Nigerians were gregarious and happy. Hands were shaken and conversations begun before the worship began.

The three of us had expected the service to be high Anglican. It was fairly low-church. That was fine. But half way into the service, during a long extemporaneous pastoral prayer, the tongues began. Not from our Nigerian friends. They were as surprised as we were.

The speaking in tongues turned into singing, and the unusual harmonies and cadences of singing in tongues drifted around and through the traditional architecture of the old church building. The tongues seemed to have both freedom and dignity and flowed easily around the Gothic arches of that old church.

I had experienced tongues on many occasions. I've been fascinated, amused, sometimes repelled, but never inspired. This time, the tongues had a dignity – a place. They had not become an end in itself. They became another way for the Spirit to communicate. And I was spiritually warmed.

Not long afterward, the priest invited the Nigerians to sing. This had obviously been prearranged, because a leader stood up and all the Nigerians stood up all around us. There we were, three Canadians right in the middle of a Nigerian choir.

We couldn't understand their words any more than we could understand the strange words of the singing in tongues. We didn't need to. We could see their faces glow, and their bodies move as they sang their faith with everything they were. It was genuinely beautiful. Again, the Spirit used them to communicate. And I was spiritually warmed.

At the end of the service – the Eucharist. Nothing unusual about it. Words I had come to know and expect. Liturgy I had come to know and expect. But again, the Spirit used that familiar Eucharist to communicate. And I was spiritually warmed.

We had coffee afterwards, my two Canadian friends and I, and two Nigerians who had been sitting near us. The Spirit, it seems, had reached them too – through the traditional liturgy, the charismatic speaking and singing, the Nigerians' song and the Eucharist. There was joy in that discovery, but for me, judgment too.

"You're a dry old stick, Ralph," the Spirit seemed to be saying to me, "but don't box the Spirit into your dry old dislikes and prejudices."

Maybe even a dry old stick can sprout a few new leaves.

COMMUNICATOR

Gospels
Listening
Story   Luke 10:29-37

When I was working in New York, I told a friend in the advertising business that Jesus of Nazareth was the most effective communicator the world has known. "The first three Gospels are terrific case histories of effective communication," I said.

"Will you come to a lunch meeting next week and explain that to a group of my colleagues?" he asked.

I gulped, because the statements had come right off the top of my head. I wasn't sure they were true. But by the time that meeting had rolled around, I was sure.

Christians study the first three Gospels to learn about the teachings of Christ. They might also do well to study the methods he used. In that group of advertisers, even the atheists acknowledged that Jesus was a "terrific communicator."

Let's look at that story we often call "The Good Samaritan" and analyze the techniques Jesus used. You could do the same sort of thing with most of the parables. First of all, the Bible tells us Jesus was listening. He was in dialogue with a lawyer. And even though the lawyer was trying to score debating points, Jesus took him seriously. He didn't give him a theoretical description of a neighbor even though he could have, and it would have been easier. That's what the lawyer probably wanted, so he'd have something to argue about. Instead, Jesus used the opportunity to tell a story.

It's not the theory of neighborliness that worked. It's the story of a neighbor and what that neighbor did.

COMMUNION

Bread
Emmanuel
Eucharist   Matthew 26:1-26
Food   Mark 14:22
Sharing   Luke 24:13-35, 22:19

I have sometimes said that to be a Christian you have to like casseroles.

I'm only half kidding. Any congregation I've ever been part of had potluck suppers from time to time, and the staple of those potlucks is casseroles. I am firmly convinced that more "communion" happens in the church halls over casseroles or at the church picnic over hot-dogs, than in the sanctuary over the ritual bread and wine.

Years ago I had lunch in a crowded Hong Kong restaurant with a missionary friend, Tom Lung, now retired in Portland. As we chatted, the waiter brought a basket of bread. Tom took one of the rolls, and without a pause in the conversation very simply broke it in two and gave half to me. That simple action, totally unnoticed by anyone else in the restaurant, turned that meal into a holy communion, as we acknowledged our mutual faith and commitment in the breaking of bread. Christ was there, present with us.

It is the most universal of human symbols. Sharing a meal symbolizes friendship and community in virtually every culture. Christians have understood the spiritual significance of that symbol and recognized that we see God in the face of other humans when we share our food and in so doing, acknowledge our interdependence.

We are not alone. To the extent that we share our bread, our wealth with others, God is with us. In that sense, the offering on the collection plate, the food we take to the food bank, our struggles for justice are all highly eucharistic.

The burden of guilt is overwhelming sometimes. The gift of guilt is that it can lead us to repentance and to the eucharistic action of breaking the systems that enslave many and engorge a few.

Christ is made known to us in the breaking of bread.

COMMUNITY

Crisis	Acts 2:43-47
Mutuality	Galatians 6:2
Need	1 Corinthians 12:12ff
Sharing	Ephesians 4:1-6

In the suburb where we lived for nine years, we were all independent. We all owned power saws, lawn mowers and step ladders. Our cupboards were well stocked so we seldom needed to go next door to borrow a cup of sugar. If there was something we didn't have, we had the money, and the stores were always open so we'd go and buy it.

And we were strangers. The only time we got together was when somebody moved away. Then we'd have a farewell party where everybody would stand around trying to think of something to talk about.

One exception. Once we had a bit of a flood after an unusual rain. The sewers backed up. For awhile, there was something we could do together. We helped each other. We got our hands dirty together. For awhile we were a community because we needed each other. For awhile we had a story, even if it was only a backed-up sewer.

COMMUNITY
Communes
Communities
Democracy
Individualism   Acts 2:43-47

About twenty years ago I produced a couple of TV programs and wrote several magazine articles about religious communities. It involved trotting around interviewing folk from various communities and rooting around in libraries.

Those were the days when bright-eyed idealists were starting communes. Some close friends of ours had thrown their date-books out the window and bundled up their families and headed out to start a commune in the Gulf Islands off the west coast of Canada. Among other things, my research was going to provide me with the material to convince Bev that we too should toss our date-books and join them.

I loved the research. I hated the conclusions I came to.

It became very evident that the only communes that lasted, were the ones that had strong, top-down, authoritarian leaders. In democratic communities where everyone got involved in the decisions, where there was no big boss, things didn't usually last. At most they would struggle along till the departure of the charismatic leader who got them started. It seemed that community and democracy were incompatible.

That put the kibosh on my efforts to get Bev to move. And I'm glad we never did because our friends left their commune in less than a year – bitter and disillusioned and poor.

Perhaps community isn't compatible with the individualism of our society. Our personal rights are paramount. Individualism infects both the right wing and the left wing of the church, even though the latter tends to use the rhetoric of liberation theology.

But liberation theology requires that we put the needs of the group ahead of individual needs. Individual convictions may be expressed, but then must give way to the will of the community.

The vision of community comes to us in glimpses. It's worth struggling toward, over and over again, even if we keep failing. It may well be the next great human achievement.

If not, it will be the next great human failure that leads to cataclysm. We will learn to live together. Or to die together.

COMPUTERS

Language	
Pride	
Technology	Genesis 11:1-9
Vocabulary	Proverbs 16:18

"So!" I said to Mark, my eldest son on his latest visit home from the university. "What are they teaching you in college?"

"Not much." My son is always ready to share his innermost thoughts with me.

"You gotta be learning something," I said. "It's costing enough."

"I'm learning languages."

"French? German? Russian?" I asked.

"No, Fortran and Cobol."

"How interesting," I said, not wanting to appear dumb. "Say something in Cobol." It only took twenty minutes to discover that Fortran and Cobol are computer languages, and that you don't talk them, you write them in strange little symbols and words that don't resemble anything, anywhere.

That was a long time ago of course. Now I have my own computer and I'm very suave and sophisticated about it all. For instance, whenever I meet someone with a new home computer I can assume an air of knowledgeability and ask, "How many "megs" does it have?" "Eight," comes the breathless response.

"Mine has sixteen," I say, "and one and a half gigs," trying not to sound too superior. Then I quickly divert the conversation to something else before they discover I haven't the faintest idea what a "meg" is. Or a "gig."

CONFESSION

Honesty
Openness
Relationships
Sincerity
Vulnerability
Witness

James 5:13-16
John 20:20, 26-29

In recent years I was involved in producing a TV program called "Celebrations," in which we told the stories of people who had been through some kind of personal hell. I became keenly aware of the kinds of risks we asked these people to take when we invited them to tell their stories of alcoholism, marriage breakdown, loneliness and death.

What was most surprising was that only one of the many people we approached turned us down. No one asked to be anonymous. We used full names and showed full faces. Their first concern was usually "Don't make a hero out of me." Gary Birch, a young football player, who broke his neck in a car accident leaving him a quadriplegic said, "Don't make me look like 'super-quad'."

We simply asked them to take a risk because those who watched the program might grow through shared experience.

We warned them they might be misquoted, misunderstood and misrepresented. All we promised was "We'll do our best to be as faithful to your story as we can."

They received many very warm letters, phone calls and personal comments as a result of their programs, often leading to even deeper contact. An unmarried mother even received an offer of marriage, which led, not to a wedding, but a very moving series of letters.

I questioned these people very directly and carefully, and as far as I can determine, no one ever regretted doing the program. In fact, most said it had improved the depth of relationships with those they loved and turned many acquaintances into friends.

CONFESSION
Openness
Sincerity
Vulnerability   James 5:13-16
Witness   Galatians 6:2

I write often for religious magazines. When I do, I invariably get a comment or two from friends in church on Sunday.

One time, Bev and I were asked to do an article called "Why We Stay Married." It involved a lot of soul searching and finally an agonized decision to do the article and to "tell all" as candidly as we could.

The Sunday after publication, there was almost a lineup of people in church wanting to talk to me, only this time the comments were qualitatively different. Sometimes with great emotion they said things like, "we saw ourselves in your story. "

Jim Taylor, who was editor of a major church magazine, tells me that stories of that kind, of people wrestling with themselves, get the highest ratings in the readership surveys.

CONGREGATIONS
Membership
Pew-sitter   Matthew 14:13ff. 11:8-17 Mark 6:34ff
Seekers   Luke 7:25-31, 9:12-17   John 6:1-13

I sometimes use the term "pew-sitter" to describe a member of a congregation. And that's part of the problem right there.

A pew-sitter is a bump on a log. Over the years I've learned to be a very good pew-sitter. I can even sleep with my eyes wide open staring straight ahead.

I don't mean woolgathering, though I do that too. Some people I know learn to "meditate"; elbow on knee, hand over eyes. It's dangerous. I tried that once, but my center of gravity was too far forward. I fell asleep and almost toppled out of the pew. You have to learn to sleep sitting up straight.

There are not as many pew-sitters as there used to be. The people who came to church just for appearances don't often show up now except at Christmas and Easter. Those of us who are there, come because we're looking for something. But we feel that if we've made it as far as the church, somebody ought to hand that "something" to us.

It doesn't work that way, at least not anymore.

CONVERSION

Born again
Cursillo
Experience
Idols
Meaning
Moderation
Narrow-mindedness

I get a little envious, sometimes, of people who have had huge, life-transforming religious experiences. But I also get sad when people are so afraid of being "born again" they keep God at arm's length.

Andy, a longtime friend of mine (so I am obviously not using his real name) had a life-transforming experience when he was in his early thirties. His life had been a mess of drugs and depression and petty crime. He got talked into going to a Cursillo, and there he "met God face to face."

It turned his life around. Probably, in the long run, it's made a better person out of him, but his wife walked out when she could no longer stand his insistence that she also have his experience. He moves from one church to another, looking for a "spiritual home" but never seems to find it.

Maybe God knew that Moses could only stand so much of God. Too much God can ruin you. When I think of Andy, I'm glad it hasn't happened to me, because I could very easily turn into a religious pain-in-the-patusche.

Andy has a problem with idol worship. He has turned his experience, or at least his perception of it, into an idol.

But that's not the problem with most of the folk I meet in church. They are running scared of overdosing on religion, so they don't want to encounter God at all, except perhaps in safe, one-hour doses on Sunday morning. They go to the other extreme and have nothing at all to give their lives meaning.

Between those two extremes, I know many folks who have been to Cursillo and similar events, and come out of them as lively, fun, active, invigorated Christians who enjoy life and live the presence of God.

"Life is a banquet," said Auntie Mame, and she might have been talking about the life of faith. But surely we can find a way to enjoy the meal and let it nourish us, without falling into the trap of either anorexia or gluttony.

DEATH
Dying
Funeral   Mark 16:1-2
Grief   Luke 24:1
Sharing   John 11:1-44

When Henry Mack died in Dumaguete City in the Philippines, there was no funeral home to take care of the "arrangements." All of us in that small Christian community stayed up the night, building the coffin and sewing the lining.

We had gone to be with Margaret his widow at the Mack home. Henry's body lay in one of the small rooms near us. We shared our sorrow and tasted our tears together. We grew in the sharing of his death, just as we had grown in the sharing of his life.

That is the way of dying in the Philippines. Death is an event to be shared. Sorrow is too precious to be tasted alone.

DEATH
Airplanes
Dying
Fear   Matthew 8:18-27
Flying   Mark 4:35-41
Mortality   Luke 8:22-25

It was a flight from New York to Toronto. A bit bumpy. Just enough to make you aware of your stomach.

Then, BAM! And a flash of brilliant light!

There were screams and gasps. Then nothing. We just kept flying right along as if everything was quite normal. Eventually (it seemed like ten minutes later) a laconic pilot spoke over the loudspeaker. "You may have noticed a slight noise and bit of a flash a few moments ago," he drawled. "Nothing to worry about. We were hit by lightning."

That's all.

Almost everyone has their favorite airline horror story. Mine involves taking a flight on FAST Airlines from Manila to Dumaguete

City in the Philippines. I took it because it was cheap. Missionary salaries didn't allow much for luxuries.

Ten minutes out of Manila, the rickety DC-3 did a sharp U-turn and landed us back where we started. The passengers were herded out of the plane, to swelter in the tropical heat with only the meager shade of the plane's wing to protect us from the blazing sun.

A mechanic eventually sauntered out of a nearby hanger, and began tinkering with the engine. Two miserable hours later, we were all herded back on board. Including the mechanic. I wondered whether I was reassured by that or not. The mechanic sat near the window watching the engine as it sputtered and spewed oil over the tropical rain forest. At each stop, he got out and tinkered.

Finally we landed at Iloilo. "All those passengers traveling beyond Dumaguete should disembark at this point," we were told. Since I was going to Dumaguete, I stayed on. One passenger. One mechanic and the crew.

And the mechanic had shifted to the other side of the plane. I wondered why.

As the engines strained and rattled over the fetid, unexplored jungle covering the mountains of Negros Island, I asked the mechanic, "Why are we not going beyond Dumaguete?"

"Because," he said, "we are having trouble with the other engine now too."

I'm always interested in what happens to me when I catch a glimpse of my own death. I remember wondering why I wasn't afraid; why I was so certain we were not going to crash. At the same time, I wondered what death in the rain forest would be like.

When we were struck by lightning on that flight from New York to Toronto, the first thing that came into my head was, "Well, if I'm going to die, I'm going to enjoy it."

That's all! And I'm still trying to figure out what I meant. But I found myself looking back over my life, and I was at peace because I knew it had at least been worth living. And a quiet, wordless prayer formed inside me. It was a prayer for those I would leave behind. It was gratitude for the life I would leave. And thanks for the life I knew would follow.

Even fear brings its gifts.

DEATH

Airplanes
Dying
Fear
Flying
Mortality
Peace

Matthew 8:18-27
Mark 4:35-41
Luke 8:22-25

I was flying out of Kelowna recently on an assignment for a church magazine. The seat belt sign had just gone off, and I was gazing at the mountain where loggers had cut huge bald spots along the ridges. The flight attendant had just started smiling her way up and down the aisle with plastic cups of lukewarm coffee, when the pilot suddenly stood the plane on its wing tip in a quick U-turn back to Kelowna, which didn't help keep the coffee in the cups or in our stomachs.

"Ladies and gentlemen," said a very flustered voice on the loudspeaker "we're going back to Kelowna, and...and...as soon as the plane hits the ground...I mean as soon as the aircraft has landed... get out as fast as you can and don't try to take any luggage or anything with you and for goodness sake, KEEP CALM" It was the longest trip home I've ever been on.

The flight attendant kept walking up and down the aisle smiling broadly through clenched teeth. Nobody was talking. Me? I wasn't frightened. I wasn't worried. Not a bit of it. I was terrified!!! Pure, utter unvarnished scared. I could feel my heart was pounding away against my ribs. I was panting as if I had just run a mile, and squeezing the armrest till it yelped.

It was a bomb scare. Some poor demented soul had phoned in a threat. And while most of us were sure it was a hoax, we were still glad the airline was taking it seriously.

A couple of hours later, after a thorough search of everything, we were on our way again. And then I had time to think a little – to reflect on the feelings I'd experienced when that aircraft was rushing home to safety.

I had been afraid all right. But after about five minutes, the terror gave way to a kind of peacefulness, and I found myself wondering if this really was the end of my life.

I was terrified of dying, but I found I wasn't afraid of death. I was grateful for the life that had been, and hopeful for a life to come. In the middle of that fear, I found peace.

DEATH

Courage
Heaven
Resurrection   1 Corinthians 15:12-57

Nature abhors a vacuum, and this is particularly true in the realm of popular mythology around life after death. Where the churches fear to tread, the popular media have a field day. There is plenty of interest in the topic, and all the stuff about angels recently has fed that interest.

So preachers are in a dilemma. Preach about it, and no matter what you say you'll be in the soup. Say nothing, and you leave the field wide open to charlatans who feed on vivid imagination and wild hearsay.

At this point I feel compelled to offer some sage advice, but since I don't have anything that feels the slightest bit sage to me, I won't. Other than to say, if you know where you are on the subject of life after death, please, for the sake of us confused souls in the back pew, preach it. If you don't know, could you do some thinking and praying and reading, so that you can help us think it through?

As more of us become long of tooth and gray of hair, our interest in the subject is more than casual. What's in store? Compost or the celestial choir?

DEATH

Faith	Resurrection	
Heaven	Retirement	Genesis 12:11
Leisure	Risk	Hebrews 11:8
Life Journey	Trust	John 3:1

There are many journeys in a life.

Moving from the tiny hamlet of Horndean, in southern Manitoba to Ottawa as a nine-year-old at the height of the Second World War is certainly one of my most vivid childhood memories. But the move was not my decision, and I was protected and loved through it all by my parents and older sisters.

The first real journey of risk for me was marriage. I lay awake the entire night before the wedding arguing back and forth with myself. I now know I did the right thing for all the wrong reasons.

And, like Abraham, I had no idea where that journey would take me. My ideas of what marriage would be like were right out of Hollywood and had no connection with reality. I also know, in retrospect, that God was with me on that journey into relationship (which I'm still on, by the way), not pushing, but offering strength. Much like a parent helping a child on the first day of school.

My second big journey was going overseas to the Philippines as a missionary. Bev and I went, cocky and naive, full of fear and bravado and found ourselves plunged into the wilderness of culture shock. Out of that frustration and struggle, we did 20 years worth of growing in the space of 5. Again, in retrospect, God was there with us, encouraging and nudging and smiling us through, holding our hands, holding our hearts and offering love, most often through the caring of Filipino Christian friends and colleagues.

Now I'm poised on the edge of another journey. Like that first trip as a child, this one is not of my own choosing. A very few years down the road will be retirement, and beyond that death. I feel both fear and faith as I approach that journey. I feel anger at the bubble-gum theology that tells me, "Give your heart to Jesus and everything will be fine."

It won't be fine. I will most likely know the pain of heart disease or cancer. I already know back pain and tendonitis and stiff joints and a host of other aches and annoyances of aging. What's probably going to be toughest for me is giving up my work. Like most males, like Nicodemus, my work is my identity far more than I'm prepared to admit. Who will I be when my mind or my body won't let me write anymore?

And yet. And yet I feel a gentle arm around my shoulder. And like Nicodemus giving up his career, like Abraham giving up his home, like Sarah giving birth in her dotage, like old Martin Luther straining away on the toilet, I can hear an inner voice saying, "It's OK Ralph. Just let go of the rail. Hang on to me. I am with you always. Oh, and Ralph, there's a beautiful surprise at the end of it all. There really is."

DEATH

Anger
Dying
Grief
Healing
Hope
Lamentation
Questions
Suffering

Matthew 5:4 (reference to the Passion Cross)

I was standing with my sister at the bedside of her son who was dying from cancer. Such a short time before, he had been playing basketball. A tall, cheerful, bright young man. And here, a skeleton covered in skin and sores was dying. It made no sense and I could feel only one emotion. Anger.

Jay had sung for years in the boys' choir at his church. And so, to his deathbed, we had called his priest, his friend and pastor. And as the priest came to his bed, I thought, "Please, don't try to be helpful. Don't try to make it right. Because, by God, it is wrong! Please don't say anything helpful."

The man was priest but also friend. He was mourning too. Perhaps also angry. And he did exactly what should be done at such times of anger and pain – he took his little book and in it found the words we needed. Not little saccharine pieties, but the huge, soul-shaking lamentations of the Psalms. With passion and anger in his voice that reflected the passion and anger in our hearts, he cried to God those vast, eternal, unanswerable questions; he threw at God the anger of our souls; he brought to God the terror in our hearts.

And the words he spoke brought peace. Not resolution. Not answers. But peace. A sense that we were part of a community that had known these things before. We were not alone. We were not the first to shout our anger and despair to God.

For that moment, it was enough. It took many quiet, sometimes tearful conversations, many prayers, many caring friends and time, to heal the wounds and make life possible again.

The "why" was never really answered. Nor could it be.

But God came into my pain to offer hope and healing. It was enough.

DECEPTION

Communication
Faking
Lies
Male
Masculinity
Men
Openness
Vulnerability

Galatians 6:2
James 5:13-16
Mark 10:35-41
Luke 24:24-27
1 Samuel 18:1-5, 19:1 et al

Bev and I had been invited to do an anniversary event for St. Andrew's, our church home for nine years in Calgary. It was wonderful seeing so many old friends. Like me, they are all grayer, balder and paunchier.

It was also frustrating, because we didn't really get to talk with any of them. At least not enough to get beyond the little verbal games we play with each other.

"Well, hi there!" He's a great big tall fellow, with a face I vaguely remember. I decide to fake it.

"Hi! Good to see you again."

"Gee, it's been a long time. How's ah....how's everybody at home?"

Now I know he's faking it too. He doesn't know who I am either. It's comforting. Suddenly a light goes on in my head, and I remember a younger, thinner face with more hair on top. We were together on the music committee. But everything else including the name eludes me. It's time to eat humble pie.

"Look I've been talking to so many old friends today, and I'm having trouble pulling names out of my head. A sure sign of senility."

"John," he says. "John Gower. And I have the same trouble, all the time." Now I have him at a disadvantage. Should I be kind, or make him squirm. I decide to be kind.

"In that case, I'll tell you who I am, so you won't have to ask. I'm Ralph Milton."

"Oh I remembered your name all right," he fibs. "It's your wife's name I couldn't dig up."

"It's Bev."

The blighter! Now he's got me squirming. I have no idea if he's even married, much less the name of his wife. I decide to use his ploy.

"So how's everybody at home?" I ask.

"Oh, just fine. Fine. Marg has decided to go back to work, now that the kids are pretty well grown." Bingo! I have her name. And I also know there's a family.

"Got any pictures of the kids?" That's a dangerous question. Some people will promptly haul out a wallet full of badly focused snapshots and you're there for an hour. This time I'm lucky.

"I can do better than that." He grabs my arm and hauls me over to the side of the room where a gaggle of teenagers is playing the kind of games teenagers play with each other. "Cindy and Elaine. You remember Mr. Milton?" They don't, and find the question embarrassing.

But I remember. It's the two freckle-faced skinny-as-a-rail gigglers I taught in Sunday School years ago.

"Holy smoke! Are you sure? Last time I saw you, you were only this high." That embarrasses them even more. So I make my exit. "Well, you're obviously busy. But it's good seeing you."

This time I take John's arm, and move him away from the teenagers. "They don't want to talk to old geezers like me, John. But it sure brings back memories. They were such bright and cheerful kids, as I remember. How are they making out?" I see the flicker of pain in his eyes and hear the slight catch in his voice before he says "Fine. They're doing just fine."

"Watching teenagers grow into adults is easily the toughest thing I've ever had to do." I can see a tear struggling for birth in his eyes.

"Look, I gotta run. Marg'll be waiting. Nice seeing you again."

He's gone. And I stand there wondering why it's so hard for men to really talk to each other.

EASTER

Providence	Luke 24:1-8
Resurrection	John 20:1-18 and other
Sunrise Service	Resurrection stories

The Winfield congregation where I worshiped for many years has a tradition around the Sunrise Service. It must be held at sunrise.

No seven o'clock soft stuff for those folks. Sunrise! And depending on when Easter falls, that can be five a.m. Which can be early and very cold, and our minister (also my wife, Rev. Bev as they called her) didn't really like the idea of a communion service in the early morning cold and fog, what with the arthritis in her fingers and all. But she wore long woollies under her gown and went, because among other things, it was her first Easter in that congregation.

The fog rolled in across the Okanagan hills. It was cold and dark and miserable as we drove toward the hillside orchard. "Should we give in and move it to the church?" people were wondering when we got there. "No," said the hardy souls. "It just might clear up."

The service began with the story of crucifixion, the darkness of the empty tomb, the despair of the disciples, and the dark fog swirled through the stories and into our souls.

Then came Mary's triumphant shout, and at that precise moment, the sun burst through the fog, and we could do nothing but grin and clap and celebrate. In minutes, the fog was gone, the sun was warming our souls, a bird was singing in a nearby apple tree and we said to each other, "Christ is risen! He is risen indeed!"

Later over hot chocolate and hot-cross buns, someone asked Bev, "How did you do that? Your timing was impeccable!"

Bev just grinned. What was there to say?

ECUMENISM

Groups	
Respect	Ephesians 4:4
Teamwork	1 Corinthians 12
Trust	John 17:23

There were about a dozen of us and we met every Thursday over a brown bag lunch. We were Catholics, Lutherans, Presbyterians, Anglicans, Baptists, Salvation Army, United Church people; some were very conservative; some very liberal; some lay and some clergy. We were an interfaith TV production group doing a half-hour program once a week.

There were only three rules: the first was that nobody had a veto; no one person should keep the group from going ahead with an idea. The second was that if two or more people wanted to work on a particular project, they could proceed, but always with the blessing, though perhaps not the participation of the rest. The third was that basic program ideas had to be thoroughly discussed by the whole group.

Sometimes the discussions were cool and considered. At other times emotions ran high and we got angry at each other.

Yet through it all, there was a fundamental respect and trust we all treasured. When we got together for a party, we had a fantastic time. When we worshiped together, we were one in the Spirit.

ENCOURAGEMENT

Anger
Civil Rights
Community
Healing   Matthew 5:43-48, 5:9-11
Hope   Luke 6:22,26-36
King, Martin Luther Jr.   John 16:33
Race Relations   Romans 8:28-39, 12:14-21

It was the Sunday after Martin Luther King was shot. We were part of a church in Teaneck, New Jersey, a church in which whites were a minority. King's assassination was a terrible blow to all of us who had struggled in the black liberation movement.

Church that Sunday morning began in chaos. The planned service simply would not do, but nobody really knew what should happen.

And then, one of the men from our choir moved quietly to the center of the chancel, and began to sing, very quietly at first, the anthem of that era, "We shall overcome."

We joined in, all of us, and we held on to each other and we sang it over and over and over, until we had sung out our rage and our fear. We sang that song until it changed from an anthem of anger into an anthem of hope. And we were healed back into a community, a community of black and white who could be together as God's people.

ENLIGHTENMENT

Call
Epiphany   Exodus 3:1-6
Experience   Isaiah 6:1-8
God, Experience of   Acts 9:1-9
Uniqueness   John 20:29-31, 20:24-25

"You mean you faked it?"

"Yeah," he said. "With everyone else in the crowd having great huge religious experiences, I felt a lot of pressure to have one too. I wanted to very badly, but nothing happened. So I invented one. Everybody thought it was wonderful. After awhile I began to believe it myself."

"I'll bet you felt really good about that."

"It's a funny thing. I knew the experience was a fake, but the feeling of God that came with the experience was real. So I think God forgave the lie and gave me the real thing instead. I guess maybe I didn't really need to fake it. I just needed to want God in my life."

I have problems when preachers start talking about "burning bush" or "Damascus road" experiences. I've never had one, but like my friend, I've felt the pressure to invent one.

Maybe some of us don't need the old two-by-four on the noggin. I've had lots of little nudgings, plenty of little aha! experiences, lots of moments when, for just a moment, I thought I caught a glimpse of God. Add them all up and I think they translate into a lot of conviction.

It just may be that God respects us enough to treat us all as individuals. All of us are unique in God's eyes. So every one of us gets special treatment.

EPIPHANY

Magi
Revelation
Vulnerability
Weakness   Matthew 2:1-12
Wise Men   John 3:16

Epiphany is the season when the penny drops. It's the time when
the world, if it pays any attention at all, says, "Ah...so!" It's a time
when a little light bulb goes on inside our head...if there is a light
bulb to go on.

That's because Epiphany is when God stages one of those
multinational show'n'tell sessions to get a simple concept
through our thick human skulls.

The concept is easy, so it's easy to miss.

God is a god of love expressed in vulnerability and weakness.
God is a god for everyone.

It's to laugh. Belly laugh even. The trouble God goes to so we
can get the point.

There is a baby. A half-naked born-in-a-barn infant with illiterate, uneducated, no-account parents. And in the door of that stinky
stable saunter these savants, proud of their pulchritude and their
PhDs. They're not only wealthy scholars, they are Gentile scholars
with foreskins intact.

There, kneeling in the cow dung, these foreign wise-guys represent the world, represent us, as by their body language they recognize a loving God in a burbling baby.

An Epiphany. A realization.

The clunk of the penny dropping.

Since the day of that show'n'tell 2,000 years ago, we've done
our best to dress up that child, to put a superman cloak on his neck
and a crown on his head and a bazooka in his hand. Then we've
shut him up in churches so he won't cause too much trouble while
we go out and ravage the world.

But once a year, if we stop for a minute after the Yuletide bac-
chanalia; stop just long enough to notice that after the smell of the
leftover turkey drifts away, there is the faint odor of camel dung
that clings to the clothing of the well-dressed academics and power
brokers we've been "entertaining" all season.

Tucked away in our deepest memories is the celestial joke, except that we can't quite remember the punch line.

Unless of course we hear it in the babble of a tiny child. Or find we're prompted by the sigh of a wrinkled woman full of years.

Then we remember.

"And a little child shall lead them."

"God so loved the world."

EPIPHANY

Children
Immortality
Innocence
Myrrh   Matthew 2:1-12

It was Epiphany Sunday. Brian Jackson of Trinity United in Vernon, B.C., was doing the children's sermon.

Brian had brought along some gold, frankincense and myrrh. He got through explaining the gold and the frankincense, though one youngster wanted to know how much the gold ring he was wearing was worth.

But the bottle of "tincture of myrrh" caused a few problems.

"What do you think this is?" asked Brian.

"Wine," said one youngster.

"Beer," opined a second.

"Vodka," chirped a third.

"I think I need to pay a pastoral visit to your parents," said Brian. He then went on to explain how myrrh was derived from the sap of trees and was about to explain how it was used in embalming bodies. He never quite got there.

"Can you drink it?" asked a small voice.

"If you do," said Brian, "It will preserve thee unto everlasting life."

EPIPHANY

Awareness
Born again
Conversion   John 3:1-10
God, Experience of   Romans 12:2

The question used to make me angry.

"Have you been born again?" I'm not really proud of some of

the things I've said to people who asked that question. Now, if I'm not too tired, and feeling good about myself, I say, "Yes. I've been born again. And again. And again."

The first time I was "born again," was the same day our first child was born. Or at least, that was the first time I was aware of God speaking to me through an event too wonderful to understand. God communicated with me through that crinkly faced child and the other children that followed.

I was "born again" the day my mother died, and the day I climbed a high mountain way above the tree line and saw a tiny tree struggling to live beside a rock in which was embedded a fossil from millions of years ago when this land had been under water.

And then there are those tiny experiences of God's presence. The Canada geese honking overhead. Rubbing the back and neck of an aching friend. Reading those old-new stories from the Bible, chuckling at and identifying with the clumsy humanity of Peter who couldn't do much except love the Jesus he would never really understand.

EUTHANASIA

Dilemma
Ethics   Exodus 20:13
Judgment   Deuteronomy 5:17
Justice   Matthew 5:7, 7:12, 22:39-40
Suicide   Luke 6:31
Third World   Leviticus 19:18

Sue Rodriguez is dead.

She had what was commonly known as "Lou Gehrig's Disease," a terrifying and incurable degeneration of the nervous system that eventually takes away a person's capacity to walk, speak, do anything except think. Sue Rodriguez fought for the right to have a doctor-assisted suicide when she felt life had become unbearable. The courts said "no."

The debate was as hot in church circles as it was in legal circles. Christians argued about "playing God," which many said was different from "imitating" God as Paul exhorted the Ephesians.

We worry about making judgments. To decide that this person should live and that person should die is a judgment only God should make, which of course implies that God actually makes those decisions.

I don't claim to know the answer to the dilemma. I do think we make those decisions far more often than we realize.

The triage in our medical and social policies, for instance.

More importantly, our international trade agreements which structure the world economy so that my country is rich because the third world is poor. My high standard living is at the expense of a family in Guatemala. My Guatemalan counterpart has a low life expectancy because I have a high one. Does the fact that I don't know that Guatemalan's name change the reality of me and my government "playing God" with a world economy that condemns that person to an early death?

If God calls us to be Christ-like, to imitate God, to break and share the bread, are we not playing God or imitating God (Is it more than a semantic difference?) to the extent that we live that call?

Sue Rodriguez found a doctor to help her die. Whether that was right or wrong, I don't know, but I do know it took courage. For both of them.

Now I wonder, do I have that kind of courage to share the bread I have so that others may live?

EVANGELISM
Commitment
Hospitality
Missionaries   Hebrews 4:2

In Dumaguete City in the Philippines, an American evangelist came to "bring Christ to the Philippines." The fact that Christ might already be there hadn't occurred to him.

He set up a tent and sent a sound-truck through the town to advertise the meeting. Everybody went. After all, what else was there to do? And, an important part of Filipino culture is to make strangers feel welcome.

After the sermon came the altar call. Everybody went forward. The evangelist was elated. And they all went forward again the next night and the next. It was the hospitable thing – the polite thing to do.

The evangelist was a member of a small denomination that operated a mission church in Dumaguete. When he went back to California, the little congregation that had hosted him continued to struggle on with a dozen people. All the "multitudes who came forward to confess Christ as their personal savior" went back to their own church or to no church at all.

In the Philippines, as here, it's a lot easier to get people to agree to something than to live something.

EVANGELISM

Communication
Conversion
Enthusiasm
Internet
Media
Outreach   2 Timothy 4:2
Technology   1 Corinthians 13:1-13

At a church conference, we were debating the merits of the famed "information highway" and the Internet. Most of the discussion was between the starry-eyed enthusiasts who were convinced it would solve all the church's problems, and the dull-eyed Luddites who harrumphed their negativity.

Those of us who are long in the tooth had a sense of *déjà vu*. Back in the fifties I was one of those enthusiasts who claimed that if we could establish radio stations in strategic locations around the world – we could "win the world to Christ in our generation." It didn't occur to us that some of those poor benighted heathens might have other things to do besides listen to our radio station, and that even if they did listen, they might not hang on every breathless syllable that dropped from our lips.

In fact, when our enthusiasm was put under the cold clear light of research, we discovered that mass media were really pretty ineffective in communicating life-changing values like the gospel, and that the thing that really worked was when the media were used to reinforce such dull and unglamorous methods as one person talking to one person.

The enthusiasts and the Luddites at our conference were both right and both wrong. The Internet is a handy tool and it's time the church learned how to use it. But it's virtually useless for evangelism.

When it comes to saving lost sheep, you have to send a shepherd out there into the bush. If you've lost a coin, you need someone with a good broom and sharp eyes. There are no technological substitutes, no high-tech solutions.

When it comes to Christian evangelism, it's the conversation over the back fence or over a cup of coffee. It's the ordinary church member who communicates enthusiasm for the gospel and the life of the Christian community. The role of the clergy is to feed that enthusiasm. The church grows when people in the church love it and talk about it.

When they stop loving and talking, it dies.

EVANGELISM
Good News
Gospel
Incarnation
Manipulation
Pastoring
Televangelism

All stories of Jesus healing
by touch and presence
1 Corinthians 13:1-13
James 5:14-16

I used to be a TV evangelist. It's true. A full-time, professional, TV evangelist. Before that I was a radio evangelist.

Now I'm a print evangelist.

My problem is that the words have been degraded. Especially "evangelist." It's come to mean more a style of preaching and manipulating people rather than simply someone who speaks the good news. I use it in its original meaning.

Every Christian should be an evangelist. Every preacher is an evangelist every Sunday morning. Or at least, should be.

I gave up on TV evangelism, not because I was bothered by the company of Jimmy Bakker and Pat Robertson (I was), but because I became convinced that what I was doing wasn't working.

Here's a story that is apparently true.

A young man asked his pastor to visit his mom in the hospital. She had a terminal illness which was progressing rapidly. When the pastor arrived, the woman was, with considerable difficulty, trying to make a phone call.

"I've been watching Pat Robertson on TV for years. He said on TV he remembered every one of us in his prayers. So I'm phoning him, because I know if he will pray with me on the phone, I'll be made well again."

When the pastor came around later, the woman lay there with the telephone on her pillow, next to her ear. "They put her on hold," said the patient in the next bed. "She's been waiting on the line for almost an hour."

As the pastor stood there, wondering what to say or do, he heard a voice on the phone. 'I'm sorry, Mr. Robertson is not available." CLICK.

The woman didn't open her eyes. "But he promised!" she whispered.

The pastor tried to talk with her, to pray with her, but she would not respond. The next day, she was dead.

"Television ministry" is an oxymoron. Well, perhaps not quite. But the pastoral part of ministry must be incarnational. Hands must be touched. Eyes must look into each other. Smiles and tears exchanged. Personal words spoken and heard.

EVE

Adam	
Awareness	Faith
Doubt	Growth
Eden	Innocence
Evil	Risk

Genesis 2:3

Sometimes I think Adam and Eve got a bad rap. Especially Eve.

In fact, I sometimes think we should move Eve right up there to top spot in the Christian hall of fame. She's the one who had the smarts to ask the world's most important questions.

Why? Why not?

Eve got herself and Adam chucked out of Eden for those questions, but would it really have been better if they'd stayed there? Did God want them to stay there?

Eden is, after all, the garden of childhood. When children don't grow, either mentally or physically, we rush them off to a specialist. God would have considered creation flawed if these creatures, created in the divine image, had not grown.

I'm not the first parent who has found the conversation of a two-year-old delightful but somewhat limited. Most of the delight in two-year-old conversations is sharing the discoveries they are making. And the main question the two-year-old asks is, "Why?" That question implies the beginning of doubts, doubts which come to full flower when the kid hits teenage.

I think God was secretly delighted when Eve picked the fruit and found the knowledge of good and evil. Eve showed a bit of gumption. Eve asked hard questions and discovered the difference between what is good and what is bad, and in the process grew one huge step towards being even more like the God in whose image she was created. God, I think, planted those holy questions in human makeup. Why? Why not?

Of all God's creatures, we are the only ones with the capacity to doubt. Of all God's creatures, we are the only ones with the capacity for faith.

So let's hear it for Eve. Without her, we'd still be overgrown kids in a spiritual kindergarten.

EVENTS

Bazaar
Communion
Community
Fellowship
Picnic   Acts 2:46
Togetherness   John 21:12

Many church leaders see the bazaars, teas, talent nights and picnics as a nuisance or, at best, a necessary break from the "real" work of the church. But what if this *is* the real work of the church? Is it possible that in the community we call the church, getting together to do these things is acting out its togetherness, its communion?

Maybe the most important eucharistic service in the church year is the annual picnic.

Just like the annual picnic, the tea and bazaar is a great time for community building. There are people in my congregation getting set up for a rummage sale. Some of them say its main benefit is the money raised. I think it'd be worth doing even it we didn't make a penny.

FAMILY

Concern
Myth
Solidarity
Worry

This story is about the night when I was very small, and Mom and Dad had gone to a wedding with Uncle Henry and Aunt Sue. They were traveling in a light cutter.

A spring snow storm blew up, as fierce and as frightening as any prairie blizzard. I was home with my three older sisters.

Verna, the eldest, had to put salt on the fire to stop the howling winds from starting a chimney blaze, so we all huddled into one bed and waited out the night. Not until mid-morning did Dad arrive to shovel out the door and come inside, sick with worry and frostbite. They had given the horse its head, and that saved their lives. The horse took them to the neighbors a half mile away, where they spent the night worrying about us while we worried about them.

The story and all its details has been told and retold a hundred times, and provided a myth that helps cement our family. We lived through that one together.

FAMILY

Compassion		
Outreach		Matthew 18:10-14
Sheep	Luke 15:3-7	1 Corinthians 12:12-13
Shepherd	Ephesians 2:19-22, 4:4-6	Psalms 68:6 (KJV)

An older child reaches out with care and love to one that is younger. And they become a family.

The gnarled hand of an elderly person reaches out with care and love to another dying of cancer. And they become a family.

The pastor listens with care and love to another tragic event in the life of a woman who has been abused, first by her husband and now by her children. And they become a family.

The young idealist risks life and reputation to reach out with care and love to an unknown person in a faraway land; the victim of an unjust system. And they become a family.

The shepherd struggles through the night to find the sheep, lost and hurt because of its own stupidity, lifts it up with care and love and brings it back to the flock. And they become a family.

A family prayer:
> O God of the whole human family,
> O God of the family called creation,
> Help us reach out with care and love,
> That we may become a family.
> Amen.

FAMILY

Deuteronomy 26:1-11, 5:16
Exodus 20:12
1 Corinthians 11:23-26

F

There are many ways to rate the success of a book. The number of copies sold is the most common (and somewhat dubious) measurement.

Of all the books published by Wood Lake Books, the one at the top of my personal "success" list didn't sell any copies at all. In fact, there are only seven copies in existence. It's called "Marieke" and it's my mother's autobiography.

During her last years, I got her writing me letters about her life in response to my questions. I strung her account together in chronological order, made a copy for her and one for each of my siblings. That little book has been read and reread by her children and her grandchildren and great-grandchildren.

Mom died within a hundred miles of the place she was born. Her life, by most standards, was unexceptional. But we read and reread her story because it feeds a deep hunger for connections, for a sense of continuity with our forebears.

I spent last summer in Israel doing biblical studies, but at a more fundamental level, it was an exercise in remembering. Just as I needed to be connected to my mother and who she was, I needed to be connected to my spiritual forebears. I needed to sit with the memory that fills every rock and mountain of that place – let that memory seep into my bones, because remembering is far more than recollection – far more than collecting old anecdotes.

Why? I look at what I've just written and that question sits out there on the end of my nose. Why?

Does it matter? Yes, absolutely. All the ancients who sat around campfires and told each other stories knew it mattered. My children knew it mattered when they read Grandma's story over and over, especially my two adopted children who carry the wounds of being torn from the heritage into which they were born.

We remember in order to learn from the past. Yes, of course, but there is a deeper reason, I am sure. I can feel that deeper reason, but I can't name it. I can sense that deeper reason, but I can't describe it.

Because another grandmother, Sophia, the spirit of wisdom, keeps whispering in my ear, "Just keep listening for the story Ralph. Just keep listening for the story."

But she won't tell me why.

FATHERS' DAY

Family	
Fathers	Exodus 20:12
Parents	Ephesians 6:1-4

Fathers' Day is a very important event that should be soberly observed in every home that has one. Fathers are a convenience feature almost as useful as an automatic dishwasher. Kids, for example, find them as useful for dispensing money as those contraptions at the bank where you can get money at two in the morning. And the only code-word the kids have to remember is "Please."

As fathers, we hold up the ideals we want our kids to live up to. We want them to have all the things we never had ourselves. Like A's on report cards. And we spend a lot of time doing the kids' homework while they are busy watching television.

Whatever time we have left, we spend trying to keep the wolf from the door and from our daughters. When we're not doing that, we're trying to give our kids good advice, which is almost as much of a waste of breath as playing a saxophone.

Sooner or later the kids learn how to be good sons and daughters, but not until they become parents themselves. By the time a man realizes that his father was usually right he has a son who thinks he's usually wrong. In fact, it never occurs to a boy of eighteen that some day he'll be as dumb as his Dad. Never mind. Somewhere along the line there should have been a test to check our qualifications for fatherhood, and probably we would all have flunked.

Our fundamental defect is that we want our kids to be a credit to us. Our parents didn't manage that, and there's no reason we should expect it.

All we can do is try to live like the Dads our kids thought we were, before they became teenagers.

FEMINISM
Femininity
Gender
Jesus
Macho
Masculinity
Strength   John 11:35
Tenderness   Luke 19:41

F

Sermon
Seasonings

69

As Rosemary Haughton points out in her book *Tales from Eternity*,
Jesus was a sissy. There's no getting around it. He cried in public,
he loved flowers, he liked to play with babies, and when people
came up and said insulting things, he'd give gentle answers.

Jesus was not your typical "he-man." He was singularly lacking
in "macho." In a real sense, he was "gentle Jesus, meek and mild,"
even though I've always disliked that phrase. It's true, Jesus spent
40 days in the wilderness and for that he had to be physically tough.
He could get mad and drive out the moneychangers.

That's not the point.

The fact is that a very important aspect of his personality was
what our culture would probably describe as "feminine." As Rosemary says, "no progress can be made in holiness, by either the individual or the churches, unless both men and women are willing to
release the captive princess, the 'feminine' side of human nature."

Of course it's wrong to call certain qualities "feminine" and
others "masculine." They are all human qualities and exist in both
sexes. But the idea that real strength is found in tenderness and
weakness is, I think, central to the concept of what it means to be
Christian and what it means to be fully human.

It's an idea that scares many men silly. It threatens all our
cultural ideas of what "masculinity" really means.

FESTIVALS

Belonging
Community
Heritage   Luke 4:14-30
Home   Matthew 13:54-58
Identity   Mark 6:1-6

In the rural Philippines, every barrio has its own fiesta every year. For one week, everyone celebrates. Even those who have moved off to the city and become thoroughly urbanized and educated, still head back to their own home barrio for fiesta.

That time is important.

There's often too much wasted in a fiesta. People who can't feed or educate their kids properly, blow a wad at fiesta time.

They roast a whole pig and invite everyone in sight; everyone, including foreigners like me. They eat too much "lechon" and drink too much "tuba"; there's lots of dancing and speeches; speeches that go on forever. It seems important that they be made, not that they be listened to.

When a Filipina goes back home for fiesta, she knows where she belongs. She might be a delegate to the United Nations discussing the fine points of world government, but when she's home for fiesta, she knows who she is and where her first loyalties are.

The barrio is home. And as Robert Frost defined it; "Home is where, when you have to go there, they have to take you in."

FUNDAMENTALISM

Attitudes
Correctness
Evangelical
Inclusiveness
Judgment
Language   Matthew 16:13-20
Liberal   Luke 9:18-20
Maturity   Mark 8:27-30

It will come as no surprise to you that my theological cubbyhole would be somewhere to the left of center. So I am pointing the finger at myself as well as many others when I say I'm getting pretty sick of the left-wing fundamentalism growing in the so-called "liberal" churches. By that I mean people who sit in judgment of any person whose theology they consider "inadequate." It gets a bit ludicrous when people are excluded because their theology is not "inclusive."

Recently I came across an article I had written some 20 years ago. I cringed at the theology, the language, the political stance. If I'm still around, I will cringe 20 years from now if I read this little diatribe.

"Who do you say that I am?" Jesus asked.

The personal response each of us offers to that question is found in the authenticity of our lives. It is our very personal response. I cannot understand yours, much less judge it, nor can you understand or judge mine.

That's why Jesus told Peter to keep his trap shut. And in the end, he had just one thing to say to Peter and the others. "Love one another."

GENDER
Culture
Female
Feminine
Love
Male
Masculine   John 4:9

I remember walking down the street with Ernesto, the first time he took my hand. I was terrified! Embarrassed. Yet I couldn't pull my hand away because in terms of his Filipino culture, it was a natural expression of affection. For Ernesto it had no homosexual overtones. It was as natural as a handshake.

I didn't pull my hand away, and in the course of five years in the Philippines, I learned to take the hands of male friends and to enjoy the friendship and the love that gesture expressed.

Later, I had some more cultural learning to do. Nilda was in my office when the news came. Her father had died after a long illness. She wept from grief – relief. Because we were good friends, and because I wanted to share her grief, I put my arm around her.

I felt her stiffen. A look of shock came over her face. In terms of Filipino culture, that was a blatant sexual advance. You simply did not touch, except in formal handshake, a person of the opposite sex to whom you were not related by blood.

Several years later, our jet touched down at the Vancouver airport. We were met by a gaggle of relatives, including my wife's cousin, Louise, a delightfully warm person. She threw her arms around me and kissed me. I froze, just as Nilda had done.

Here I was, back in Canada, and my reactions were all Filipino.

GENDER

I've been reading a lot of "men's" stuff recently. It's about whatever we call the male issues in feminism. And that's taken me to digging into the research on gender differences.

Surprise! Women and men are different. *Viva la difference!*

But guys, I don't know how to break this to you. What they've been finding out about gender differences is good news in the short run, but in the year 2020, women will have a decided edge. That's because all the things men do best and most easily can now be done by machines. Mostly computers.

All of this is in very general terms, of course, because there's a huge spectrum of characteristics within both men and women. In a room full of people, the tallest person may well be a woman, but on the average, men are taller. If you put Margaret Thatcher and Jean Vanier on a male/female characteristics continuum, Vanier would be well on the female side and Thatcher well on the male. But we're talking averages here, which means we have to be very careful not to put individuals in pigeon holes.

So. Men, we generally do better at things involving muscle bulk, hand-eye coordination and rational, logical, left-brained calculations. Women, you most often do better at understanding and, if you choose to, manipulating human relationships. Also at communicating ideas and concepts (as opposed to facts). Guess who has the upper hand in the new millennium? All of this is proving scientifically what we've hunched all along. When Bev and I go out for an evening with friends, she picks up all kinds of subtle information that I don't even notice. When it comes to understanding other people, I am, as the PCP's (politically correct people) say, perceptually challenged. Or as they said in Jesus' day, I was born blind. I simply don't see the hurt in people's eyes. I simply don't see the anger under the calm exterior.

Which, if you think about it, may mean that virtually all our leaders are blind to the most fundamental issues of human welfare. They can't see what it is that Jesus was fussing over. Show them an oppressed person, and they see an economic or political problem. They don't see a hurting human. It's no good yelling at them. They were born blind.

Which does not mean they cannot be given sight. It takes a miracle, but miracles do happen. There are thousands of men who have learned to see, or if they cannot see, at least to trust the judgment of someone who can.

John Newton was born blind. He became a successful slave trader, who saw the African people only as a commodity to be traded and used. Then amazing grace burst into his life, and he was given the gift of sight. One day Newton looked into the eyes of one of his slave cargo and saw a human being, a child of God.

Years later, he wrote:

"I once was lost, but now am found.
Was blind, but now I see."

GIFTS
Gratitude
Sensitivity
Thoughtfulness
Unselfishness   Luke 21:1-4

Ivan Cumming once told me a bit of his story that helped me understand that no gift, however small, was rejected by God.

The year was 1933. The great depression was underway.

His father sat at the kitchen table with nothing to say. The barn had burned down. Now the six-year-old boy could feel the despair, as he had felt the heat from the burning barn a few days before. Ivan took 38 cents from his piggy bank, and slipped it into his father's callused hands.

"Thank you, Son!" his father said.

GOOD FRIDAY

Despair	Lamentations 1:12
Easter	Matthew 26:ff – 28:10
Futility	Mark 14:43 – 16:8
Resurrection	Luke 23:1 – 24:12
Suffering	John 18:12 – 20:18

It was a cold Good Friday morning. We were huddled in the churchyard of the tiny Anglican community in Westbank, B.C. It used to be out in the country, but now it is right beside a major highway, and the roar of traffic almost drowned the voice of Rev. Doug Hodgkinson.

"Is it nothing to you who pass by..." Doug almost shouted out of his prayer book. It seemed so futile. The folks in the cars hardly gave us so much as a glance, as we shivered our way through the liturgy, as we straggled back into the sanctuary, leaving our big wooden cross out there beside the road for people to ignore.

Liz (Doug's spouse) and Doug, and Bev (my spouse) and I went for lunch after the service. I shared my sense of futility. All of us felt it. But then Bev thought of some of the folks from her United Church congregation who had come that morning to put words around their pain. That cross meant something to them. And they would be there Easter morning.

Doug talked about people from his parish, and the painful journeys some of them were walking. They had come. And they would be there Easter morning to hear and sing the next chapter in this universal drama of dark to light, of death to birth, of despair to hope.

It was nothing to those who passed by. And for a time, I felt only despair for our struggling churches, and I was ready to suggest to Bev and Doug they pack it in, give up the ministry and find some useful occupation.

But some were there. Bev and Doug saw their faces. They saw the tears, but in those tears they saw reflected the first warm ray of resurrection.

I needed my fellow disciples, to point it out to me. Or I might not have made it back to sing the song on Easter morning.

GOOD FRIDAY

Easter	Matthew 26:14-16, 47-50
Pain	Mark 14:10-11, 43-46
Suffering	Luke 22:3-6, 47-48
Suffering Servant	John 13:21-30, 18:1-3

There is, in Jerusalem, a church called Saint Peter in Gallicantu. It is the site that commemorates the betrayal. Tradition has it that this church is built on the site of the house of the high priest Caiaphas where Jesus was taken after his arrest (Mark 14:53) – where Peter denied him.

Like so many of the churches of the late Byzantine period, this one owes its existence to the piety of pilgrims rather than historical evidence. But we went there, not because it was the actual place, but because for generations, pilgrims have gone there to remember the betrayal, to remember the suffering of Jesus.

Deep down below the church is a cistern carved into solid limestone. To make it easy for modern pilgrims, a stairway has been carved down into it, but during the time of Jesus, there was only a hole, about two feet in diameter in the top.

The tradition says Jesus was lowered down with ropes into that cistern, and that he spent the night there in the basement of Caiaphas' house. Certainly the evidence of suffering is there – iron rings, where people were chained to the wall for lashings – inscriptions carved by desperate prisoners. This was certainly a place of suffering, and therefore a good place to remember the suffering servant.

We stood there for awhile as our instructor pointed out the historical evidence, or lack thereof. But then we stopped the wonderings of our minds and allowed the imagination of our hearts to connect us with the pain of one who suffered there for us. We sang a hymn about suffering, and spoke some prayers, but mostly we were silent in the presence of the mystery.

I sat down by the wall. I looked up to the circle of light in the hole above me. I wondered what Jesus felt, thought, feared, hoped on that dark and terrible night. I tried to feel that in myself, but couldn't. I had no bloody whip marks throbbing on my back. I knew that in a few moments I would mount those stone stairs to safety and a good hot supper.

G

Sermon
Seasonings

75

So I don't really understand the pain. I've never been there.

Can I really know the resurrection, if I have not known the pain that leads to crucifixion?

GOOD FRIDAY

Death and dying
Grief   Matthew 26:36-46   Mark 14:32-42
Hope   Luke 22:39-46   John 18:1

My friend is dying.

He has leukemia, a cancer of the blood stream that slowly, day by day, is eating his life away.

He's facing his death head on. He's never run away from death before. He's seen it in friends and family and associates. He has cried at many gravesides and wept with many friends in grief.

So for him, death is no friend, but it's not an unknown enemy either. It's not a taboo subject in the family. Death can be faced. Prepared for. Death will bring pain, but it will not bring final destruction. It will hurt, but the hurt will heal.

Nobody welcomes pain. But if we hide from it, it sneaks up and hits us where we are most vulnerable. If we close ourselves to the grief, it will fester inside and destroy us.

Of the many gifts offered by our faith, one of the greatest is Good Friday. On Good Friday, if we allow ourselves to enter the grief, to know the pain of death and separation, then we also experience the great joy of Easter. Easter means little without Good Friday.

My friend with leukemia has known many Good Fridays. You see, he's a medical doctor who cares very deeply about his patients. And when they die, as all of them will at some time, he grieves for them and for their loved ones.

Now it's his time. His time to grieve for himself, for his family. Because he has learned the art of grief, Good Friday will not destroy him. Or his family.

For them, there will be a joyous Easter morning.

GRACE
Baptism
Love   John 1:12, 16

The power of what we call "grace" struck me one day in church when the minister was baptizing a baby. Talk about undeserved love! That brand new baby couldn't do much besides fuss and cry, smile a little, eat a lot and wet her pants.

Her Mom and Dad beamed down at her with nothing but love in their eyes, and all of us in the congregation smiled and felt a bit of that love too. As the minister sprinkled the water on her tiny head, made the sign of the cross on the child's forehead, kissed her gently and handed her back to her Mom, all of a sudden I knew deep down inside what the minister meant when she talked about "grace."

GRIEF
Appreciation
Joy   2 Samuel 18:33, 1:17-27
Laughter   Genesis 37:29-35

Last summer, I held a very close friend in my arms as he sobbed at the news that his son was dying. Over the months that followed, we grieved together, he for a son and I for a friend.

My friend's grief was deep and terrible. But sometimes in the grieving we'd remember his son's delightful humor, his penetrating wit, and my friend and I could laugh a little through our anger and our tears.

We didn't laugh to deny the magnitude of grief. We didn't laugh to avoid the pain. We laughed, because not to do so would have denied the beauty and the joy of a young man we loved. It would have denied the loss we were grieving.

GUILT

Birth
Choice
Christmas
Parenting   Luke 2:41-52

I'm a grandfather in waiting.

By the time you read this, the child will have been born, and we shall, I trust, all be rejoicing.

But this is being written near Christmas when the child is still a gentle swelling of the belly and a gentle swelling of the light of hope in my daughter and son-in-law's eyes. It is written at Christmas, when I can see a small evergreen decorated with the memories of childhood dreams. A shell from our first lonely Christmas in the tropical Philippines. Six popsicle sticks glued to-gether as a star from a Christmas event at church. A garish ugly star proudly purchased from the first five dollars earned by shoveling snow.

But hidden in the memories is the stab of excruciating pain that cannot be named here because that would be to break a confidence. Of many nights of anxious waiting. Of sudden fear that turns, over time, into a dull but ever present ache.

And guilt. Are current problems rooted in our family past? Of course.

Were Bev and I good parents? Was I a good father? A good husband?

Who can bear to ask such questions?

We make choices through our lives, and each choice excludes all other choices so we never know what might have been the better course. Such as it was, our life has been our offering of ourselves.

We walked along our creek today, Bev and I. There along the snow-covered bank, a young couple and a child were feeding ducks.

We took our children out to feed the ducks. We have that memory decorating our own tree of life, and I will stand by that. We could live on guilt and fear and anger, but I'll settle just for this.

We took our children out to feed the ducks.

GUILT
Forgiveness
Repentance
Sin

John 1:8-9
James 5:13-16

Frank McNair is my friend and psychiatrist. In a conversation recently, Frank said the greatest medical advance of the past decade was the recognition by the medical community that human beings are a single unit. Humans are physical, psychological, social and spiritual creatures, but the divisions between those are quite arbitrary and they are really completely connected.

That doesn't come as a huge surprise to those of us in the Judeo-Christian tradition. Our priests and prophets have been saying that for centuries.

At the moment of that conversation, I had a mild infection in my right eye. "Is that infection psychosomatic?" I asked.

"At some level, yes," he grinned, "but if you came to see me with it, I don't think I'd start asking you questions about your childhood."

But he might have. The sty in my eye got started by a bout of the flu, and the flu was as bad as it was because I was run down, and I was run down because I'm a workaholic, and I'm a workaholic because way deep down inside I still think I have to earn my salvation, and I caught the bug because I work in an office where lots of other people had the bug and where people reinforce my workaholism.

It's all connected.

It's not hard to get a sty in the eye treated, but a tear in the eye may be much more difficult. Tears of guilt, especially.

There are bushels of books in the pop-psyche shelves prescribing ways of escaping guilt, but most of them miss the point. Guilt has many forms, of course, and some of it may be misplaced. But sometimes guilt is the Holy Spirit saying to us, "You have sinned. And you are in need of forgiveness."

Psychiatrists, no matter how skilled, cannot offer forgiveness, because psychiatry is amoral. It doesn't know about sin. But psychiatrists like Frank know that sin is real – that the guilt resulting from sin is a gift of God, that the sin and the guilt must be taken seriously and named as such. Repentance, turning around and changing what needs to be changed is the response the Spirit of Guilt demands, and in return, offers the graceful gift of forgiveness.

This is priestly medicine. Only in the community of faith is it understood and only there can it be practiced.

GUILT

Incentive
Motivation
Stimulus   John 2:1-11

I have a friend who works in the headquarters of one of the major denominations. He and his co-workers had Bible study together once a week. "Glad to hear it," I said.

"It's awful," he complained. "The Guilt-Trip-of-the-Week. Every Tuesday, a new guilt trip. That's not what Christianity is about."

This summer, I was sitting beside Bev on our back patio. She had a stack of professional magazines for clergy beside her. "I never seem to get around to these during the year," she said.

"Why?" I asked.

She sighed. Bev knows a fair bit of psychology. "I guess I didn't want to badly enough to make time for them."

With her comment in mind I began idly flipping through the magazines. I was a bit concerned because Wood Lake Books, the publishing ministry I work with, had produced some of them. Why did Bev find reading them a chore rather than a pleasure?

I remembered the comment of my friend from church headquarters. I was startled, then dismayed at how many of the articles in those magazines laid a guilt-trip on the clergy who read them. "You're not doing it right!" they seemed to proclaim.

Of course we are guilty. Clergy are guilty. Laypeople are guilty. Far too much and far too often.

But any educator will tell you – guilt works with children only in the short run. In the long run it backfires. If you want to be a leader of children, you need to find other ways to motivate. The people who hear sermons and the people who preach them are children too, and the same educational principles apply.

There are times when it's right and necessary to say, "Look folks. We blew it! We're in it up to our eyeballs, and it's time we drained the swamp!"

People will work together to drain that swamp if they like each other, if they are a community, if they've had a bit of fun together and if they have a cheerleader who pats them on the back with regularity. And that only happens if we take a break from time to time to have a party.

Guilt will start them draining the swamp, but it'll never provide enough motivation to finish.

Maybe that's why Jesus' very first miracle was to keep the party going.

HEALING

Attitude		Matthew 22:35-40	Mark 12:28-34
Ministry	Luke 10:25-28	Deuteronomy 6:5	Leviticus 19:18

A conversation with a lawyer and a doctor recently convinced me that the church can be a most effective and subversive agent in culture by healing the attitudes, by healing the spirits of its members. The doctor and the lawyer spoke movingly of how their attitudes were healed in the church, enabling them to see their work as ministry – enabling them to fine tune their responses so that when they made decisions under pressure, as was so often the case, they would do so out of their faith perspective.

Our word "heal" has its roots in the Old English word "hµlen" which means, "to make whole." A whole person is one who genuinely loves God, neighbor and self. When worth is ascribed to one of that trinity at the expense of the others, there is a social and spiritual sickness. Sin is the traditional (and still useful) word. It's a sickness that may have physical symptoms; often psychological and social symptoms.

So I think that maybe the call to our disenfranchised minority church, the "faithful remnant" if you like, is to look to the New Testament church and relearn the faithful art of healing.

HEALING

Faith		Matthew 9:1-7
Holism		Mark 2:1-12
Wholism	Luke 5:17-26	James 5:13-16

In his book *The Uncommon Touch* Tom Harpur echoes the call of writers such as Norman Cousins and Bill Moyers and the experience of people like Wayne Irwin of the Lowville Prayer Center in

Burlington, that the *cri de coeur* the churches must hear is for healing. Not the showbiz stuff of TV evangelists or the mechanical ministrations of the medical establishment nor even the analysis of the social activists.

It springs from the growing awareness in many disciplines that everything is connected.

The human body is not simply an organism. It is also a soul. That comes as no surprise to people of faith, but the idea is being rediscovered by medical practitioners and social scientists. The whole world is one interconnected system, and there is something holy about it that must be loved and guarded and healed.

So when a group of HIV positive people gather at the Roman Catholic Cathedral in Toronto, or some middle-class folks come together at the Lowville Prayer Center, or when a group of my friends practice Healing Touch therapy with a friend about to have a mastectomy, and they pray specifically for healing and their clergy leads them in a ritual of healing, they are part of what may be the most important social-political-religious movement since the Reformation.

And probably the least understood.

HEALING

Action
Leprosy
Spiritual   Luke 17:11-19

A colleague said to me the other day, "The social action of the church is disintegrating."

She may well be right. And perhaps it is because we, as the church, have been trying to fix things instead of helping people heal. The job of the church, the vocation of the saints, is in healing attitudes – healing relationships.

Medical science can fix leprosy (Hansen's disease), which affects the nerves in the skin – the sense of touch. It is the insensitivity that causes the injury. The physical curing of leprosy is relatively easy.

There is a far more profound social and spiritual leprosy that attacks the sensitivity of the soul. The nine lepers went to the local outpatient clinic and got a quick cure for their physical leprosy. But one who was outcast because of where he was born – this one came for something more than a cure.

He came for healing, and it was given joyfully.

HEROES

Jesus
Myth
Strength   Matthew 4:1-11
Superman   Mark 1:12-13
Weakness   Luke 4:1-13

One of the archetypes that appears again and again is that of the great hero, the superhuman, who comes into some desperate situation and saves the day; the white knight or the cowboy in the white hat.

Not all these hero tales are destructive by any means. We can choose to enjoy the stories of Ulysses, King Arthur and Wyatt Earp simply as stories.

But when we come to archetypes like Superman, we can call it entertainment till we're blue in the face. The fact remains, as *Time* magazine put it, "They have become jerry-built substitutes for the great myths and rituals of belief, hope and redemption that cultures used to shape before mass secular society took over."

The obvious parallels between the story of Superman and the story of Jesus are too many and too close to be accidental.

But the danger, I think, isn't in seeing Superman as a kind of quasi-Christ. It's in seeing Christ as a kind of Superman who runs around setting things right for the world.

The value of looking at the hero archetype in folk tales and in contemporary mass entertainment is to appreciate again what Jesus was not like; that he was instead a "man of sorrows" who suffered and died.

HOME

Church
Mothers
Refuges
Risk
Safety
Security

Ephesians 2:19

I watched 14-month-old Jake (my spiritual director) on our back porch yesterday. It was one of those lazy warm July days. We had a little plastic pool with two inches of water, and Gran (Bev) and Kari (Jake's mom) and I sat with our feet in the water and drank ice tea while Jake, in beautiful, innocent nakedness splashed in the pool and toddled from point to point across the porch.

Jake did his first real walking just a week ago. He'd toddled a step or two before that, but he saved his first major solo flight, all the way across the living room, for a day when Gran and Gramps could watch and celebrate.

But on the porch yesterday, I noticed that Jake always picks his destination – something he'll be able to hold on to – before he sets out on, what for him are major journeys. Jake is not yet totally convinced that walking is a natural thing for humans to be doing. He feels more comfortable with this bum-sliding substitute for crawling that he perfected.

In the middle of the afternoon, Jake and Gran went for a bit of a nap. When she brought him back out, Jake headed right for the safe haven of his mom where he snuggled for a few moments before resuming his affair with a world that has entirely too many table edges just at the height where they hit him on the forehead.

I bump my head more often than Jake, I think. I go out on trips and make brave speeches and undertake all sorts of daring-do, and get myself into bushels of trouble. But I always know that I'll be home a week Tuesday. Like Jake, I don't start out till I see a place to hold on to. I sleep more soundly when I'm home and Bev is there asleep beside me. If I'm going to have a headache, I'll wait and have it when I'm home.

Jake and I and everyone everywhere need a home. The problems of our life don't change much as we grow. Except we don't have mom around. But we still need a home. That's where God and the church come in.

HOPE

Conviction
Faith
Storytelling
Understanding   Romans 1:8-17, 10:9-17

If I have heart problems, one of the medications the doctor may prescribe might be simple aspirin.

Now the doctor might well argue that aspirin was developed as a pain killer and was not originally intended to be used to prevent blood clotting, and therefore shouldn't be used to treat sick hearts. The doctor may explain that to me in great detail, which will impress me with the doctor's great learning, but won't do much for my sick heart.

Now if the doctor had simply said to me, "This will help your heart. But did you know it'll also help your headaches?" then we would have combined her learning and my need in a way that would bear fruit (to mix the metaphor just a little). And if my doctor then tells me stories about others who have taken aspirin and it's helped them, and if she occasionally tells me stories about her own struggles and pain, then I'll leave her office with a sense of hope.

Oh, and did you know that a number of tests have shown that when a doctor believes in a medication or procedure, the probability of it being effective is greatly increased?

I'll bet that applies to pastoring too.

HUMILITY

Authenticity
Pomposity
Simplicity   John 1:14

A friend and I walked wide-eyed into the massive front doors of the sparkling modern church. The narthex was larger than most churches we knew.

A solemn usher in a morning coat escorted us to a pew.

Up front there gleamed row upon row of organ pipes, and the music, a little oversweet but well done, clung to us as we lowered ourselves timidly into the plush padded pew.

All around us were women in fur stoles and men in expensive pinstripes. At exactly 11:00, the organ sounded a brilliant trumpet fanfare and the choir, rich in maroon robes, began the procession. They looked impeccable. Their singing was impeccable. The entire service was impeccable.

A boy soprano sang a solo. His bell-toned voice rang through the perfect acoustics. His diction was, well, impeccable.

Then, for just a moment, he forgot the words. He was embarrassed and afraid, but for me it was the best part of the service. Up till then I'd felt left out. I had been talked at and sung to, but the moment the boy soprano forgot the words, I shared something with him. I knew how he felt. Instead of being just a performer, he became a human being like me. That was in Florida, just before Christmas.

The next Sunday I went with Bev, my wife, to a service at Red Deer Lake where she was the pastor. It's a tiny church; a hundred people and it's jammed. The paint on the floor is worn and it has a tiny little electric organ with one small speaker.

It was the annual Christmas concert. The kids tripped over the bathrobes and towels in the Nativity pageant. The farmers and ranchers were there in their blue jeans and jackets. The gentle smell of hard work and cow manure suddenly triggered something in my mind.

"Jesus would have felt very much at home here," I thought. "He would have had a marvelous time right there, in the front row, listening to the kids lisp and stumble their way through the story of his birth."

In the big church, we heard a lot of words about God. In the little church, the Word became flesh, and dwelt among us.

HUMILITY

Perspective	Mark 9:14-28
Pride	Luke 10:17-20

As miracles go, it doesn't rank with the parting of the Red Sea or changing water into wine. But I hunch the broken biffy aboard the Columbia space shuttle was a miracle. A very small one, but a miracle still.

Or maybe it's a very small heresy. You tell me.

Every once in awhile, when humans, either individually or

collectively, get swelled heads, something happens that makes them aware of their humanity. The American establishment is certainly very proud of the technological accomplishment involved in Columbia. Maybe they should be. But it seemed to be a bit of divine poetic justice when those superbly trained astronauts in a billion dollar craft had to contend with a busted biffy – a punctured privy.

I thought it was hilarious. I'll bet God did too.

HUMILITY

Family
Perspective
Pride   Luke 1:52

Maybe God doesn't always "put down the mighty from their thrones" quite the way we expect. A few years ago, after boasting to my wife about a new promotion, my daughter (who had been listening with very mild interest) walked up behind my chair, ran her finger around the edge of my bald spot and said, "Dad, you've got a hole in your head."

I don't think she was trying to bring me back down to earth. I don't even know whether God was, but again, I think God had a chuckle over it. In fact, I think maybe that's why God planned for teenage daughters.

HUMILITY

Perspective   Luke 1:52
Pride   Ephesians 4:1

It was at a big mission conference in Chicago. We were in one of those big old churches, the kind with the long center aisle slanting down to the front, the kind brides love to walk down. We were to see a film, but the projectionist didn't show up. The chap in charge of the program asked me if I could run a projector.

"A piece of cake." I said. "Sure."

Hundreds of people had gathered and were waiting. The church was full. To fill time while I was threading the projector, the man went up to the pulpit and started saying how grateful they were to have the "audiovisual expert from New York" to help them out. He used that phrase several times. And I'd be lying if I said I didn't enjoy it.

Now, you know that little toggle thing on the front reel of a movie projector, the one that holds the full roll of film in place? Guess what I forgot?

The lights went off, the projector came on, and the front roll of film flipped off with a great clatter and unrolled all the way down the long, sloping aisle to the front.

I turned the projector off. The lights came on again just in time to reveal a red-faced audiovisual expert from New York winding up the film from the front of the church to the back.

Following the film, there was a closing meditation. The scripture? You guessed it. Mary's poem, from Luke. "God has put down the mighty from their thrones.

HUMOR
Attitude
Perspective

Humor has been defined as tragedy plus time. The tragedy and stress of this past year will be in perspective ten or twenty years from now. Then, we may be able to laugh at least at some of what has happened. And perhaps see God's hand in the rest of it.

Sometimes, for some people, that time can be foreshortened. Sometimes we can gain that perspective even while the wounds are still throbbing.

Here's an idea that sometimes works. Write a short history of the year you've just lived through, but do it from a perspective of twenty years hence.

Do a time-warp with your brain. Try to imagine what it will all look like then. Twenty years from now. Parts of it may be hilarious. All of it will be less painful. At some points, you may see the hand of God.

It certainly works for me. Well, sometimes. When I'm ready to stop feeling sorry for myself. When family or work problems seemed overwhelming, I've been able to find a few gems of gentle humor while sorting through the crud.

Sometimes I lie in bed and fantasize myself writing a learnèd historical treatise for the most learnèd of Learnèd Societies. It's hard to keep track of footnotes when you're lying in bed, but no system is perfect.

There comes a moment when it's time to stop licking our wounds and get on with being the church. The church is not the church without a sense of perspective, a sense of humor. And dare I say it? Christians are not Christians without a sense of perspective, a sense of humor.

What the heck. The above exercise loses you nothing even if it doesn't work. If it does, it might just drop a bit of the load from between your shoulder blades.

You may not tiptoe through the tulips but you might be able to lift your head enough to see the horizon.

HUMOR

Laughter
Prayer
Wheatley, Willis (Artist)   Psalms 126:2

There is strength in weakness. A clown has no power, no authority and can demand nothing. But a clown can help us get our pretensions into perspective, can help us see ourselves as we really are. The clown speaks to the child in us, and that child may tell us the truth.

In my days as a semi-militant atheist, I was dragged one day to an event in the basement of a local church. I can't remember who dragged me or why, but I do remember being angry for allowing myself to be talked into this waste of time.

I also remember a speaker. Not his name but his jokes.

They were good spicy, gutsy stories and we all laughed until we literally ached. Then just as the laughter reached a peak he burned a sentence into my memory, "If we know how to laugh, then we also know how to pray. Let us pray!"

That man shattered my image of Christianity. To suggest an intimate relationship between laughter and prayer didn't at all correspond to what I thought these people believed... a stuffy grandfather in the sky who mostly said, "Thou shalt not!" Maybe that's why the incident flashed into my memory when I first saw a drawing of Jesus by Willis Wheatley; Jesus with his eyes twinkling and his head back in wide-open laughter.

Wheatley called the picture, "Jesus Christ, Liberator." I've loved that picture ever since. Laughter is an essential ingredient of freedom.

Wheatley's drawing always seemed to represent the opposite of the desperation Kahlil Gibran described when he said, "They shall laugh, but not all of their laughter. And they shall cry, but not all of their tears."

HUMOR
Dance
Laughter

I still smile at the laughter we shared one New Year's eve at a church party. Kari, my teenage daughter, and Gus Spohr, a six-foot-six, former "Mountie" did an exaggerated, crazy Latin dance across the gym floor. Their ability to laugh at themselves and to have us laugh with them was a sign of emotional and spiritual health.

There's something very fundamental about a sense of humor. I think it helps us know we are human, to know how far short we fall of any "ideal," and all we can really do is depend on God to accept us, "just as we are."

HUMOR
Fool
Foolishness
Laughter   1 Corinthians 4:10

Conrad Hyers says in his book *Holy Laughter*, "the absence of humor and the loss of comic perspective, signifies the pride symbolized by the fall, and comedy a reminder of paradise lost."

Unless our stories are told with a deep, very basic sense of humor, we can easily turn them into idolatry. We can be trapped by the pride that makes us believe the stories are more important than the people who tell them or hear them; that the stories themselves are "sacred" and should not be soiled by frivolous giggling.

Humor, on the other hand, helps us see ourselves as essentially just a little ridiculous; helps us know that we often do dumb things and that part of our story will always be a little bit stupid and pointless. I like Paul's term, "fools for the sake of Christ."

"A common trait of dictators, revolutionaries and ecclesiastical authorities alike," says Hyers, "is the refusal both to laugh at themselves or to permit others to laugh at them." In other words, they're afraid that if people laugh at them, they might discover their humanity and their nakedness. Remember *The Emperor's New Clothes*?

HUMOR
Laughter
Wheatley, Willis (Artist)

Real laughter; deep, human, caring laughter is a moral and religious necessity. When we lose it, then the things we believe very quickly degenerate into bigotry and hatred. Søren Kierkegaard says that the more fully we live, the more we discover the comical. Then he goes on to tell us that nobody believes things more deeply and intensely than someone with a religious faith. That's why it's more important for religious people to have a sense of humor than anyone else.

Humor is a very serious matter. When I look into the eyes of the laughing Jesus in Willis Wheatley's drawing, I also see in them a deep caring. Without that deep caring, laughter is cynical and destructive, as it so often is in ethnic or sexist humor. It is the difference between laughing *at* people or *with* them.

I can almost hear someone muttering . . . "I suppose I've got to draw a laugh every 20 seconds when I get up to speak!" Not at all. You may very well give a deeply moving talk about a very serious subject, never drawing a smile from your audience and still show a deep sense of humor. It has far more to do with attitude than with laughter.

HUMOR
Attitude
Envy
Greed   Psalm 126
Laughter   1 Corinthians 12:4-13
Pride   Galatians 5:22-23

There's much in life that isn't funny. Horrid things happen. Look in any direction and you'll see people fighting with each other. Look in our own homes and see us fighting for our emotional, spiritual and physical lives!

There are many reasons why there's so much pain.

One of them, a small one perhaps but important nevertheless, is the lack of humor.

I don't think I've ever heard a sense of humor numbered as "a gift of the spirit" in church or anywhere else. But it most surely is right up there with patience, trust and caring.

Our sense of the ridiculous has much to do with our creation in the image of God. Of all God's creatures, we're probably the only ones given the gift of laughter.

Our Reformation forebears made a big mistake when they kicked laughter out of the liturgy. Humor has plenty to do with virtues such as faith, hope and love. Humorlessness is reflected in such sins as pride, greed and envy.

Religion is a laughing matter.

And humor is a pretty religious business.

Our mouths were full of laughter
and our tongues sang aloud for joy.
(Psalm 126)

HUMOR

Attitude
Church
Laughter
Perspective
Problems

Ten years ago I was asked to write a weekly humor column for our local newspaper. I set myself the task of finding some problem or annoyance being faced that week by myself or by the town as a whole. I resolved to fuss around till I saw something funny in that problem.

One of the first things I encountered was the water supply. Once a year, the pine needles in the mountains turn the water a deep brown and everybody grumbles. Sitting in that water having a bath, not sure if I was getting cleaner or dirtier and not enjoying the process one bit, I decided the people of Winfield needed to laugh about this. The result was a whole series of columns around the "tea on tap." I rang a series of changes on that theme every spring when the water turned brown.

Having sung the praises and benefits of this "tea," I began to fantasize the benefits. I even had one column about an evangelical realtor volunteering to baptize a prospective customer in the brown liquid of the toilet bowl.

The result? The townspeople had a bit of a chuckle, got together and laughed over their frustrations, then did something about it.

As for me, I learned how useful and healthful it is to discipline myself to seeing the fun in ordinary garden-variety problems. Especially the ones that afflict the church.

As someone has said, "The church is like Noah's Ark. If it wasn't for the storm outside, you wouldn't be able to stand the stink inside."

HUMOR

Clowns
Foolishness
Fools for Christ
Perspective   1 Corinthians 4:9-13
Preaching   Ezekiel 37:11-14

Humor in sermons has hardly anything to do with trotting out a few jokes to get the folks' attention or to spice up an otherwise dull narrative. That's a writing and a theatrical skill which is very useful if used well and appropriately. But it doesn't have much to do with a genuine sense of humor. It is possible to be very funny while being totally cynical and cruel.

Humor starts first of all with our own theology. It starts with perspective.

Unless we first of all see the homily as an utterly ludicrous, audacious, heretical act, and ourselves as arrogant and nervy, we will not ask forgiveness for even having contemplated the idea that we had anything to say about God.

We know our arrogance is forgiven by God and by our community. Still it seems inconceivable that a human would have the temerity to write about God or speak of God from a pulpit. And yet knowing that – nevertheless, even so and notwithstanding – we are called.

Called. Not necessarily capable or wise or clever. Just called. God help us, we of all people are called to preach the Word. It's crazy, but there it is.

We will put our feet in our mouths. We will fall flat on our faces. Like the clowns we are called to be, we will stand up, dust ourselves off, and do it all over again. I'm convinced there is no better metaphor through which to understand the preaching ministry than that of the clown.

There's a cosmic joke in the act of preaching or writing. Unless we catch the point of it, we will in fact be self-serving egotists striving for our own personal gain. And the Good News will not be preached.

The clown offers a delightfully liberating image. The omnicompetent, professional, status-seeking preachers, relying on what's in their heads and on their bookshelves, gain exactly what they seek. Admiration and status. "Verily, they have their reward."

The fools for Christ who understand the joke work just as hard and faithfully at their preaching. But they do it hoping for nothing more than perhaps an understanding hug from someone when it's done. They know that the results of preaching don't have that much to do with the sermon anyway, so they leave it up to the Spirit.

The essence of homiletical humor is not sidesplitting yarns or sharp one-liners. Homiletical humor is a fundamental awareness of the grand, glorious improbability of it all; of the lip-smacking ludicrousness of a Gospel that is "foolishness to the Gentiles" and any other rational, clearheaded thinker. The delight of it all is that rational, clearheaded thinkers sometimes believe it. And live it. They bet their lives on it.

The word humor has to do with moisture. The preacher who doesn't get the point of that joke is as dry as Ezekiel's bones. But can those bones live?

Yes. Humor is partly caught and partly learned. But it takes a little believing first.

HUMOR
Divine Gifts
Gifts
Jesus
Laughter

The Jesus who cried and laughed was crucified. The Christian church has reflected much on the Jesus who wept but only rarely on the Jesus who laughed.

We are children of a compassionate God who weeps and dies with us. We are children of an angry God who struggles with us for justice. We are children of a fun-loving God who laughs with us.

The church has had lots to say about the first two. Not much about the third.

A two-sided Trinity lies pretty flat.

IDEALISM

Justice
Peace
Silence
Verbosity
Words   Micah 6:4

At this moment, I'm thinking I should go join a Trappist monastery. I'll even throw my beloved computer in the trash can and recycle all my books and other papery paraphernalia.

They say the things you love are the things that will frustrate you, and this is certainly true of words. "Words, words, I'm so sick of words," said Eliza Doolittle. And just at this moment, my eye fell on a banner in my office that says, "Without justice there can be no peace."

"What in blazes do those words mean?" my inner cynic shouts. Many of my friends use the phrase, "It's a justice issue!" as the *coup de grace* in any argument about what should or should not be. But what is a "justice issue"? Those at polar opposites in the abortion or death penalty debates would both claim they were on the side of justice.

And what is peace for that matter? The *Pax Romana* of Jesus' day was both peaceful and just by Roman definitions. When Ferdinand Marcos ruled the Philippines with his "bolo democracy," some Filipinos said, "For the first time, we have peace in the land."

Words! Bah! Humbug!

What about a moratorium on words? A silly suggestion.

Here's a better one. What about a moratorium on definitions?

Better still. Suppose we stop using words as knives to slice reality into neat little pieces we can label and control and just start acting on what we already know.

Best suggestion of all. Not a single one of the preachers reading this will pick it up, unless we have a few Quakers among them. This Sunday, no sermon. Everyone sit close together, hold hands, and let's just be with each other in silence for 15 minutes and think about those words, "justice" and "peace" and how they are lived in our own personal lives.

IMMANENCE
Art
Communication   Isaiah 57:7
Meaning   Romans 10:15

On the mantel in our house sits a prize ebony carving I brought back from Tanzania. It's the figure of an old man bending under a heavy bundle. In the face of that old man I see a deep beauty; the beauty of years of suffering, of hope. His face says what I would like my face to say when I am 90 plus.

I don't know who did the carving. There's no signature on it.

It was bought from a Belgian priest who was involved with a cottage industry project where the carving was done.

That carving communicates something to me, something I can't put into words, something that wood carver may never have imagined. I think it's a work of art, like a dance by Anna Pavlova. Someone once asked her to explain the meaning of a dance. She said, "If I could have said it in words, I wouldn't have danced it."

INCLUSIVENESS
Inclusiveness
Political Correctness
Sexism   Galatians 3:26-29

There's a very small book that has been on the best-seller lists for months now. *Politically Correct Bedtime Stories* (James Finn Garner, Macmillan, 1994) is good fun, and readings from it make lively entertainment when groups of socially aware folks gather.

Such was the case the other night at our house. It got us wondering what "politically correct" Bible stories might look like. The story of Abraham's circumcision, told with strict political correctness, provided a good hour of absolute hilarity.

Garner takes political correctness to its *reductio ad absurdum*. I've never heard "political correctness" defined, actually, but at its best I think it represents a valid and worthy concern to use language in an inclusive and responsible way. But correctness and conformity sometimes become ends in themselves, and hence a bit silly. Then the best corrective is a good laugh at ourselves.

Those of us (preachers and writers) who use words professionally, have a particular responsibility in this struggle. We have a responsibility to use our language justly, thoughtfully and well.

I am not speaking only of "sexist language" though that is part of it. I am concerned about our thoughtless attitude toward language, even by folks who are very ready to "fix" the sexisms they encounter.

Many of us are guilty of cavalier substitutions of generic terms for masculine terms. We've all generated our share of hymns or texts where "he" and "him" have all been changed to "God" so that the word "God" occurs many times in one ludicrous sentence. I've even been guilty of that linguistic aberration, "God's self." We remove the sexist bumps in the road and substitute linguistic potholes.

Exclusive language cannot usually be fixed. It must be translated. Inclusive language is a new language and it takes work to learn it. We can't change "brother love binds man to man" to something like "sibling love binds person to person." That turns poetry into doggerel. The whole verse needs to be rewritten, from the ground up.

It's a literary rule of thumb that the more specific the word, the stronger it will be. Turning "man" to "person" does not make the term more inclusive. "Person" is a generic term that includes everybody in general and therefore nobody in particular. Women have been marginalized by our language, but inclusiveness will come when women are named as often as men, not when we've turned our language a generic gray.

In the wonderful "Servant Song" in *Songs for a Gospel People* the editor, Gerald Hobbs, achieved inclusiveness, not by changing "Brother, let me be your servant..." to "Sibling, let me be your servant..." but by using "sister" in one verse and "brother" in another.

Inclusive language is like all good writing and speaking. When it's done well, most people don't notice it.

INCLUSIVENESS

Metaphor
Myth   Genesis 2:46ff
Political Correctness   Genesis 6 – 9
Sexism   All of Jesus' story parables

The most difficult part of the language problem is in the area of myth, metaphor and story. It is virtually impossible to communicate anything except an abstract, depersonalized philosophy without using myth, story or metaphor. But they are notoriously specific and therefore reek of exclusivism. That is why *Politically Correct Bedtime Stories* by James Finn Gardner is so funny. When you sanitize those myths of their particularity, they become ludicrous. When the fairy godmother becomes "a paranormally skilled deity person" the story dies.

Stories and myths (including biblical stories and myths) deal with specific characters in specific times and situations. They may well be archetypal images, but these images come to us as specific women, men, children or animals in specific circumstances and places. Cinderella is the archetypal "youngest child" who prevails in spite of the evil machinations of family members, but the story cannot be told in any generic way. The story cannot be told except through its sexist and classist assumptions. Take those out and you kill the story.

Metaphors are by definition exclusive. For instance, any metaphor we may use for God – mother, father, brother, sister, parent, friend – has a negative connotation for somebody. Even "God" is an English word and probably not acceptable to those who would prefer Allah or Manitou. But deity or higher power are too abstract to have much meaning for anyone. The more abstract and "inclusive" the term, the more likely nobody really feels connected.

INCLUSIVENESS

Bible	Ruth 4:5
Language	Luke 13:10-14
Race	Mark 14:3-9
Sexism	John 4:5-9, 8:1-11

Richard Tarnas, in *The Passion of the Western Mind* argues that it is impossible to describe ancient Greek philosophy in inclusive language. Greek philosophy is solidly based on a patriarchal world view, and if we are to understand that philosophy we must describe it in patriarchal language. We can no more use inclusive language than we can change their use of the plural "gods" to our monotheistic "God" without being highly inaccurate in our description. Using language appropriate to the world view being described does not mean endorsing that world view, but simply acknowledging it.

Tarnas' argument might well apply to our use of biblical language. Are we perhaps trying to promote the fiction that biblical society was inclusive? Is this kind of historical revisionism honest?

Women, children and non-Hebrew races are badly treated in the biblical record. Let's not pretend it was otherwise. But let us make a particular effort to find the stories of women and children and non-Hebrews that are there, and use them as imaginatively and creatively and as often as possible.

The storytellers and redactors who selected and edited the biblical text purged their names and the stories of these neglected people from the record. Let's acknowledge that historical reality, and then go on to correct the problem. Let's get creative and energetic and tell lots of stories and develop many new metaphors which are focused on the ones who were left out of the biblical saga. Which of course is exactly what is happening in feminist literature. Let's do more of it.

INCLUSIVENESS

Language	John 15:15
Political Correctness	Ephesians 2:11, 19
Sexism	Ecclesiastes 7:5

"What do you guys want for dessert," she asked. "Oops, I forgot. I'm not supposed to say 'you guys' anymore. What do you folks want for dessert?"

"'Folks' makes us sound like doddering octogenarians," he said.

"All right. So what would you 'people' like for dessert?" she asked through partially clenched teeth.

"'People' is too impersonal. Too detached."

"Humankind?"

"Likewise too detached. Impersonal."

"Friends," she smiled as best she could. "What would my dear friends like for dessert?"

"Too intimate," he said dully. "You hardly know us."

"Idiots," she yelled. "What do you idiots want for dessert?"

"Judgmental," he said.

"I give up. You come up with a usable alternative, or there's no dessert."

"Y'all."

"Huh?"

"Y'all," he said. "Free trade with the Americans. A good non-sexist term for a group of people. We can import it from the deep south. What could be more inclusive than 'Y'all'?"

"Y'all go and soak your head," she said. "Y'hear?"

INDIVIDUALISM

Community
Mutuality
Salvation   Romans 12:4-5
Support   1 Corinthians 12:12ff

As we begin to anticipate the year 2000 and reflect on this past century, it seems to me its greatest sin is easier to spot than its greatest virtue.

That sin is individualism.

The idea that a human exists apart from clan or community or relationship has helpful aspects. Modern psychiatry emphasizes "individuation," a sense of your own identity, as necessary for emotional health.

But the same concept creates loneliness, aimlessness, frightening insecurity and a moral vacuum.

Christians and Jews have always been strong on community. The modern aberration of right-wing born-again "just-you-and-me-God" religion is not Christianity. There is no such thing as individual salvation. God's call in the Bible, God's promise of salvation is always offered to the whole community.

We visited the giant redwoods on a trip to California recently. These magnificent giants stand as much as 300 feet tall. They're hundreds of years old. How do they survive that long? How come the strong winds blowing off the Pacific Ocean don't topple them?

A signboard in a park provided the answer. Giant redwoods seldom grow alone. Their shallow root systems spread out and intertwine with the roots of the other giant redwoods, and in that way they support each other. That's why giant redwoods grow in clusters. They need each other for mutual support.

INTELLECTUALISM
Challenge
Evangelism   Matthew 4:19
Outreach   Mark 1:17

There are many versions of this story. Some say it's really about evangelism. But basically it goes something like this.

There was a group that called themselves, The Fishers Club. In their club headquarters, there were fish symbols galore, hooks and nets and floats and rods.

All the members of the club wore old hats with fish lures stuck in them, and tall wading boots which got quite uncomfortable on warm days. But they were proud to be fisherfolk and so never took them off.

They had a well-stocked library of books about fishing. And several times a year they ran seminars to which noted world fisherfolk were invited to come and deliver learnèd lectures. All the talk and all the activities at the club centered around fishing.

But then one day, the club had a new member. They had not had a new member for some time, so this was a unique experience. And the new member asked an interesting question. "When do you go fishing?"

Well, it turned out, the members of the Fishers Club had never actually caught a fish. In fact, they had never actually seen a live fish. And the idea that they should actually go out there in a boat or wade into the water came as quite a shock to them. They had long meetings on the subject and eventually came to the conclusion that the new member would have to leave. The new member obviously knew very little about what it really meant to be a member of The Fishers Club.

INTERDEPENDENCE
Community
Insurance
Risk   1 Corinthians 12:12
Sharing   Ephesians 4:25

I had a friend who was in the "big leagues" of mountain climbing. He led the first climb up the southwest face of Mount Logan, probably the toughest climb in North America.

When he and his climbing party go up the side of a cliff, they're roped together with strong nylon cord, not to tie them down but in case one of them should slip and fall. That's interdependence, and it's literally saved John's life several times.

Of course, that cord may restrict their movement to some extent. That's the difference between a community and an insurance policy.

JESUS
Communication
Incarnation   John 1:14

One of my most precious books is called *The Faces of Jesus*. It is a brilliant collection of portraits of Jesus, from across the centuries, cultures and ages. It represents the thousands of ways people have tried, through pictures and sculptures to express what they mean by "Jesus Christ." As the text by Frederick Buechner describes it: "These are the desperate, lonely, wordless, eloquent, clumsy, tongue-tied cries of the centuries."

The point of all those pictures is not whether they accurately represent what the man Jesus of Nazareth looked like.

Nobody knows that anyway. They represent the struggle of human beings to understand beyond words the meaning of that man, and to somehow communicate that reality. As we look at those images, we can share the struggle and some of the insights.

JESUS
Apocalyptic
Chosen
Jews
Messiah   Mark 13:32-37

Of course I believe in the second coming. Christ will come again. Or perhaps already has and nobody noticed, just as Jesus came to a tiny country two thousand years ago and hardly anybody noticed.

Last summer, I spent six weeks in that tiny country baking my head in the heat of archeological digs. Mostly, we (I was enrolled in the Jerusalem Studies Program of St. John University in Collegeville, MN) were studying John's gospel. I was impressed again how much

John is about God standing our assumptions on their heads.

If you temporarily set aside the lengthy sermons and discourses, John becomes a story of reversals, of the least likely people becoming instruments of God's redemption. Mary of Magdala is the outstanding example. In fact, I began to wonder if perhaps she was the mysterious "disciple whom Jesus loved."

"How odd of God to choose the Jews," is a little rhyme that kept coming into my head. How odd of God to choose such a bungling race of misfits as the people of the covenant. How odd of God to choose a Nazarene artisan. How odd of God to choose a funny little Jewish sect that told unlikely stories of miracles and resurrection and made fools of themselves speaking in strange tongues.

How odd of God to choose a woman like Mary to bear this messenger. Mary, who sang a song about a God who "put down the mighty from their thrones," and lifted up those "of low degree."

So of course I believe in the second coming. But if God is consistent, God will confound all our predictors, Hal Lindsay and me included, and be among us in a way that none of us expect.

So as Jesus says in Mark, "Keep awake." And keep looking deep into people's eyes. You may be talking to the Messiah.

JESUS, MISSION OF

Children
Christology
Learning
Openness
Spirituality   Matthew 15:21-28
Woman at the Well   Mark 7:25-30

It's easy for an old curmudgeon like me to get jaded doing Bible study.

It's easy to begin to think you've heard it all, and you don't expect to hear anything new, so you don't.

Then ka-zing! Somebody says something and the windows open and the cool, fresh breeze blows in.

That happened in Calgary when one of the people in a "Dancing with the Text" study group said the Canaanite woman opened Jesus' eyes to his mission to the world outside of the Hebrew faith. Not only that, she went on to say that it was precisely Jesus' openness to the woman that was a mark of his divinity.

Being a naturally skeptical type, I've been under-whelmed by arguments of Jesus' divinity based on the miracle stories. I've never had problems with the resurrection, but my affirmation of that doesn't have much to do with the "evidence." It's not his absence from an empty tomb that convinces me, it's his presence in my empty heart.

But now suddenly, something I find deeply convincing. I've always been moved by Jesus' claim that unless I become like a child, I will not know God's Shalom. And children are open. Children know they don't know and are ready to receive, to feel, to touch, to listen, to grow. If Jesus is saying that the child in me is closest to the heart of God, then Jesus must have felt that was also true of himself.

Sister Corita once said that the most theological of all words is "Wow!" I have no idea what the Aramaic equivalent of "Wow!" might be, but if Jesus could say, "Wow! That's right!" in response to the insight of a poor, desperate, marginalized foreign woman, then the heart of Jesus was very close to the heart of God.

Suddenly this jaded curmudgeon is excited about the Bible again.

JOY

Advent
Choice
Disillusionment
Experience
Happiness
Hope
Preparation

The classic line from the old "meller-drammer" has the suitor pleading with Dad for the hand of his daughter. Dad gives in. "Take her, and make her happy."

Daughter squeals her delight, races into her lover's arms, and they live happily ever after.

It don't hardly happen that way no more.

Daughter has discovered she doesn't belong to daddy, and more importantly, that her handsome hero, no matter how muscular his biceps, can't make her happy.

I can't tell you how many fantasies I've had about promotions I desired or achievements I struggled for, knowing that if I got it, I would be happy. Doesn't work worth a hoot.

I knew when we got married that it was my job to make Bev

happy. I didn't manage that. Then I hoped that my children would make me happy. They didn't.

Now finally after six decades of looking for something or someone to make me happy, the penny drops. If you want something like that done, you've got to do it yourself. Only I can make me happy.

And that is doubly true of that uniquely Christian concept of joy. I've never yet come across a definition of joy, and that may be because joy can't be defined. It can be experienced. I experienced it at the bedside of my dying brother, as I sat there, crying my eyes out, trying to focus on a snapshot of my infant grandson.

Joy and happiness are not a matter of ignoring pain and singing loud choruses of "Look on the sunny side of life..." Running away from pain may postpone it a little while, but it'll get you far worse in the end.

Joy is a baby born in a stinking stable. Joy is the cry of hope from the mouth of an infant, as you sit there up to your backside in cow manure. Joy is looking at a picture of your grandson while your only brother is dying.

It is far easier to focus on the crud. On the dying. On the pain. But the choice for that deep form of happiness called joy is the choice to hear the baby, to focus on the snapshot, to hear the voice of God over the noise of the traffic.

It takes some doing, but it's there. And learning how to do that is the task we face during Advent.

JOY
Dance
Holy Spirit
Rejoicing   Matthew 5:23-24

I was teaching a course in radio broadcasting at a school in Nairobi. One of the students was an Anglican priest from Nigeria. His name was Jeremiah.

Jeremiah had life and exuberance and joy. Which is not to say he couldn't be sad. I saw Jeremiah editing a taped interview with a mother who lived in the slums of Nairobi. Jeremiah was weeping.

One day I was helping Jeremiah record a program of African religious music. He was in the studio. I was in the control booth.

As we copied each record to the tape, Jeremiah was up out of his chair, dancing all over the studio. He would never quite finish his dancing in time to get back behind the microphone to announce the next piece. So we'd have to stop the tape, get him seated, and start in again.

Later, over supper, I chided Jeremiah gently for running over the allotted studio time. "It was your dancing that did it."

He looked at me with a mixture of laughter and sadness in his eyes. "Ralph, the missionaries came to Africa and told us the story of Jesus. But they only told us half the story. We read the Bible and found the other half. Jesus wants us to dance.

"In my home, when people come to church, they all walk toward the church dancing.

When they come to the altar to bring their offering, they are dancing. If they are not dancing, we tell them, 'go back, find out what is wrong with your life and make it right. Then when you are dancing, come back with your offering.'

"We have a gift for our white brothers and sisters. It is dancing. When you have learned to dance your faith, then you will know the whole story of Jesus."

JUDAISM

Heritage		Deuteronomy 6:4-9
Shema		Luke 10:27
Tradition	Mark 12:29-30	Matthew 22:36-38

I only brought one thing back from Israel for myself. Aside from a head full of new ideas and insights.

When I returned from six weeks of study, I brought for myself a mezuzah, the little container which practicing Jews nail to their doorpost and which contains the Shema. I nailed it to the doorpost of my home in Kelowna. And I found myself filled with deep emotion as I pounded those nails.

I think my feeling had to do with connections. Connections to that vast and holy tradition that was seared by the desert sun into a faith that provides the essence of life if only I could take it, apply it, believe it, live it, be it.

JUSTICE

Character
Conflict
Courage
Disagreement   Matthew 6:43-48, 6:21-24
Fairness   Luke 6:27
Weakness   Romans 12:12-13

On various kinds of conflict used in writing:

An important and difficult form of conflict is that of struggling with one's own weakness. This kind of dramatic tension makes good reading and good watching, but is much more difficult to write. It requires a far deeper feeling and understanding of human nature. And when those stories are real, they may tell us more than we really want to know.

From this kind of conflict comes some of our finest literature. Just think of Shakespeare's Hamlet, or Chekhov's short stories, or Jane Austen's novels. And of course the Bible is full of such tension.

I think I was about nine years old, living in Ottawa, when I had my first personal encounter with this kind of conflict. For reasons I can't recall, Jimmy Bennett and I had been having a running battle. A group of my friends had grabbed him and were holding him so that I could sock him in the nose. I didn't do it.

I'm not sure what my motives were then; fear perhaps, but I know what they were later. I didn't hit Jimmy because it would have been a cowardly thing to do.

My father had been watching this through the window and praised me with great enthusiasm for my "courage" and "strength of character."

LAITY

Bible Study
Congregations
Lay Ministry
Leadership
Preaching

There's a church not far from here that doesn't invite me to preach anymore. I'm not sure if they are embarrassed, or have had a change of heart because of what I said, or are just plain mad at me. But they don't invite me back.

I'm kind of an ecclesiastical hermaphrodite. I'm not ordained, but then I've been hanging around clergy and church things for so long, most people think I am. I don't even blink when I get letters addressed to "Rev."

As a result, I get to preach quite often. And the congregation in question had a minister who was away quite a bit for some good and some not so good reasons, and so they invited me to come and preach, again and again.

Then one day I fired a sermon at them, which asked in very plain language, why some of them were not preaching once in awhile. I speculated on the reasons. For some, getting up and talking in public wasn't even conceivable. Fine. Preaching was not their calling. Fine.

But I happened to know of at least a handful who regularly spoke in public. Why not in church? Was it perhaps because they didn't know enough about their faith? Were they embarrassed to show their ignorance? Then, I said, get off your duffs and do something about it. Learn. Study.

I wasn't quite that blunt, but almost. My sermons are not noted for subtleties.

I haven't been back since. I have heard that they now have an active Worship Committee, and that some of the lay folk in the congregation take services now and again. Was that because of my outburst?

I'll never know.

LAITY
Congregations
Leadership
Clergy
Risk
Courage   Luke 10:1-11, 17

Some time ago in Teaneck, New Jersey, Bev and I were part of a church where there was a gap of about a year and a half between clergy. It was a tough time for the congregation, but also a good time, and a number of very capable leaders came out of the woodwork. The church was considerably stronger at the end of that time.

An interesting thing happens with us lay people when you

back us into a corner and make us take a bit of leadership. We scramble around and bellyache like mad, but in the end, we find some words for our faith that we never knew we had. We begin to articulate things we've felt, because we've had to root around in the Bible and other resources. We'd rather learn a little than make fools of ourselves.

If I ever get to be in charge of anything in the church, I will pass some kind of edict that says one Sunday a month the preacher goes on retreat and the service is done by the lay people. (I realize that in some denominations that goes against the rules, but rules can be changed.)

That could just turn out to be the best evangelistic strategy in the book. Jesus took a gang of 70 lay people without training and said "Go!" No prepared scripts. No predigested sermons. Just "Go!" And at Pentecost, God sent the Holy Spirit to that group of lay people and said, "Do it!" And they did.

LAITY
Community
Listening
Liturgy
Ministry
Sermons
Worship   1 Corinthians 12:1-end

On listening to a sermon:

Trudy Steber is a counselor in the public school system. Each day, she deals with the problems and possibilities of growing up in a changing society. Not only does she exercise her ministry as she works with youngsters in the school, she has a special gift to bring to the church, and a unique contribution to make to the sermon.

Another person in our congregation is Ron Harrison. Ron is a mechanic. He knows a lot about how people like me feel about our cars; some of the idolatry and anxiety we bring. He has a ministry to me through his work as a mechanic, but he also brings that ministry into his sermon listening. Cars are powerful symbols in our society. Ron knows something about that; probably more than I do.

Salley McFadyn is a homemaker. She knows a lot about children, their problems at school, at play and in the family. She knows the pressures and tensions that go with being a neighbor, a homemaker, and the special pressures of being a woman. She has a ministry in her family and her neighborhood, and she has a special story to bring as her contribution to the sermon.

LAITY

Congregational Responsibilities
Creativity
Liturgy
Sermons
Worship
1 Corinthians 12:1-end

We're learning new things in our churches about the ministry of the laity. If lay people do really share in the ministry of the church, and if part of that ministry is the worship service (including sermon), then we have a responsibility to make that worship work.

I believe it does work (or can) more than most clergy believe. But I say that, partly because many sermons have been very meaningful to me and to others I've spoken to, and partly because I have some background in communication skills and theory.

Mind you, I've sat through some colossal flops. Many of those flops have been as much the fault of the congregation as the preacher. As lay people, we need to do some work to find out what we have to bring to the worship event. It's never occurred to most of us that we do anything more than get ourselves into church, then sit there and say, "do it to me!"

LAUGHTER

Community
Spontaneity

I remember a church service, years ago. The ushers had just taken up the offering. They were walking down the aisle when one of them tripped on the pile in the carpet, and sent his offering plates and those of his partner flying in a flurry of envelopes, dollar bills and quarters all over the front of the church.

The congregation sat in stunned silence.

Then the minister said the only thing that could be said. "For goodness sake, laugh."

And they did.

Till the tears rolled down their faces. And while they laughed, they got down on their hands and knees and picked up the money, put it back on the offering plates, and carried on with the worship service.

LECTIONARY
Curriculum
Preaching
Resources
Spirituality
The Whole People of God (curriculum)   Ephesians 4:7-8

There are undoubtedly a number of ways in which preaching can spring out of the life and struggle of a congregation. One valuable tool is the Lectionary and one case-in-point is *The Whole People of God*™ curriculum.

The phenomenal success of that curriculum is not that it follows the lectionary. Or that the writers and editors have great skill. Or even that it's intergenerational. All those are major contributors, but not the central fact.

The curriculum works, I'm convinced, because those who do the writing and developing are mostly ordinary church folk who gather first as a community to wrestle with the Bible passages. They ask the very simple question, "What is this passage saying to us, right now?" Only after they've heard that word do historical-critical concerns of biblical exegesis come into play. Used too quickly, scholarly insights can be a barrier rather than a window.

That's not all. When a lectionary-based curriculum like *The Whole People of God* is used in the church school, and the entire community focuses on one theme, the minister and the study group are not the only ones looking at the scriptures for that week. The Sunday School teachers should be looking at it. Children will know that their parents are studying the same parts of the Bible as they are. Families are more able to talk with each other and with their minister about their faith journey. Interesting relationships, ideas, "aha's" keep bubbling up throughout the community.

One clergy friend told me recently, "We were taught in Theological School that preaching should arise from the pastoral experience, but we were never really told how to do this. Now, the lectionary and the curriculum give us a tool."

The alternative? Peaceful coexistence. An understood pact

between preacher and congregation. Nothing really relevant is said and nothing really relevant is heard. Nothing much happens.

Or worse. The "pastoral relationship" becomes a tennis game. Clergy vs. congregation. Clergy always serve the ball but always miss the court. Congregation never get to return any balls. Score: 0-0.

I feel very strongly that the lectionary is a gift of the Spirit for our society in this time. Maybe not every society and probably not for all time. But right now, the lectionary is a powerful instrument for both prophetic and pastoral ministry when clergy and congregation explore it together.

LEISURE
Free-wheeling
Relaxation
Summer   Mark 2:23-28
Vacations   Exodus 20:8

Well, it's the middle of summer.

The congregation is sparse because half the congregation is away doing what all of us would like to be doing in mid-July. Goofing off.

I heard of a well-known theologian who claimed he spent two months one summer and didn't think about God once. Knowing the man, I find that hard to believe. But does vacation, for deeply religious people, mean taking a vacation from God?

Well, that's a little hard to do, at least if we believe that God is with us all the time, whether we're aware of it or not. But maybe we can take a little vacation from the heavy-duty ways we often think about God. Maybe we plug up our spiritual plumbing with all that hard work and profound thinking.

One summer, Bev and I were sitting on a beach – she with a batch of theological journals she was trying to catch up on – me with a bunch of books I had bought during the course of the year, all of them "serious" reading. At one point we realized we had spent several hours there, and neither of us had looked at either book or magazine. We'd simply sat and soaked in the sun and let our minds free-wheel.

We talked about it over lunch and tried to recall what it was, exactly, that we had been thinking of. Neither of us could remember. But we felt relaxed and refreshed, both physically and spiritually. So who says God wasn't part of that daydreaming?

The congregation in the pews this Sunday is mostly the regulars. They are, generally, the "old faithful," those for whom church is a lifetime habit. Many of them are active, hard workers in God's vineyard.

Maybe this might be a good Sunday just to tell them to relax. Let their minds and their lives free-wheel just a little. Take a break from trying so hard. Give God a bit of room to work.

LIBERALISM

Attitudes
Conservatism
Education
Language   1 Corinthians 13:1

Among the things that sometimes divide, sometimes unite, are the little linguistic telegraphs people use to identify themselves into groups. Snippets of King James English curiously mixed with middle-class slang and even sometimes a bit of mild profanity characterize the evangelical end of this spectrum. I like the delightful phrase I heard from one preacher. "I'm gonna give 'em hell, the Lord willing." When charismatics pray there's the whispered, "Thank you, Jesus," and hands held up to receive the Holy Spirit.

Christians close to the liberal end of the continuum find "religious" language embarrassing except in worship or formal occasions. They speak about "God" rather than "Jesus" and their language is sprinkled with words from Jungian psychology and liberation theology. Words like "liberation" and "revolution" make evangelical Christians uncomfortable, just as phrases like "praise the Lord," used outside of church, make liberal Protestants and traditional Catholics squirm.

There are also different approaches to education. Evangelicals and charismatics hold meetings and rallies where high-powered preachers bludgeon submissive followers into guilt-ridden conformity. Or so it seems from the liberal point of view.

The liberals on the other hand spend endless nonproductive hours in self-serving groupie activities, writing all sorts of nonsense on large sheets of newsprint, after which they go out and picket, start petitions or otherwise stick their noses in places about which they know nothing. Or so it seems to the evangelicals. Each group has a caricature of the other.

There cannot be understanding – we cannot be just in our assessment of each other – until we get beyond those caricatures and talk to each other like real people.

LIBERATION

I dislike the name, "liberation theology." It's far too clinical for a free-wheeling, scruffy, hands-on movement. It's a little like talking about "a committed interpersonal relationship" rather than "being in love." But I guess we're stuck with the term until somebody comes up with a name that reflects the life it represents.

Liberation theology has undergone far too much academic sterilization. A plastic imitation of what is basically a very messy but beautiful process has come to us through the scholarly literature on the subject. This literature is analytical. It's boring.

It's like analyzing a joke. When you're all done, it's no longer funny. It's not a joke anymore.

The real thing is bubbling away, often in feminist groups where people have been given permission to fall in love with the story and the song. These groups allow the story and the song to generate wild and woolly ideas, ideas and conclusions that church leaders would find "indefensible."

Liberation theology sprang up in Latin America because there were not enough clergy to go around. Clergy often started these groups but they couldn't stand over them to make sure they got it right. The clergy had to set these simple, unlettered folk free to see what they would see and to hear what they might hear out of the biblical story.

Liberation theology is giving the Bible back to the people, says Harvey Cox who has some tough words to say about this in *Religion in the Secular City*.

Protestants lost the Bible in two ways, says Cox. First, it was the historical-critical method of biblical analysis that did it to us. That method effectively took the Bible out of the hands of lay people. But instead of returning it to the priests, it fell into the hands of the scholars.

As a reaction to that, the fundamentalists came along. They grabbed it away from the scholars. They insisted that everything in the Bible had equal value, that the begats and the beatitudes were on the same level. They allowed all sorts of eccentric interpretations, reducing the Bible to what Cox calls "a kind of I-Ching." So instead of giving the liberating message of the Bible into the hand of ordinary folk, the fundamentalists bronzed it, put it in a display case, and turned it into a graven image. A talisman.

Reacting to the fundamentalists, the scholars dug in with their explanations. Reacting to the scholars, the fundamentalists claimed more and more for the Bible. Ordinary folks simply became confused and abandoned the Bible entirely.

Liberal scholars "dismembered" the Bible, says Cox, and the fundamentalists have "embalmed it." "It must be given back to the ordinary people from whom all these well-meaning authorities have removed it."

LIBERATION
Bible
Exegesis
Interpretation
Laity
Listening   Matthew 11:25
Theology   Luke 10:21

We think of liberation theology as a Latin American phenomenon, but it is happening in North American churches. It's happening in feminist groups, and among other groups of hurting souls. But surprisingly, its also happening in some pretty WASP-ish middle class suburban churches where it's probably needed more than anywhere else.

Liberation theology often happens around the lectionary. The preacher and members of the congregation sit down early in the week. The lections for the upcoming Sunday are read. "So, what is this saying to us, right here, right now, in our congregation?" That fundamental question gets argued and fussed over.

If the pastor has the courage to hide the Bible commentaries, to talk very little and listen a whole lot, interesting things can happen. There will be insights that never occurred to the preacher. There will be lots of "wrong" conclusions. People will make assumptions about the historical context that are simply incorrect. They will also make some very profound and "right" observations. The wise pastor lets the text speak first. The wise pastor knows that people must fall in love with the stories and songs. They must learn the melody and the harmony of the tradition. Only then can they do the analysis.

When North American study groups approach the Bible with this free-wheeling spirit, they are doing liberation theology. They share the basic method and recklessness of their Latin American sisters and brothers. The Spirit speaks. People respond. People act. But note that in liberation theology it's the people, not their leaders, who discern the spirit, who respond and act. By reflecting on these passages with the people, the pastor will enter into their lives, and the preaching will take on a quality and a power and a relevance that could not be there otherwise.

LONELINESS

Abuse
Addiction
Consumerism   Isaiah 55:1-2
Pain   Proverbs 9:1-6
Urbanization   John 4:13-14

Urban loneliness is a terrible thing. It affects even people living in the country, who because of highways, cars, television and money have, in effect, become urbanized.

The response to the pain of urban loneliness is usually to find a painkiller. People find many different kinds. The most socially acceptable narcotic, skillfully encouraged by the media, is overconsumption of almost anything. To fill the big black hole inside, we buy a new car, more clothes, more gadgets. Or we watch more TV or go on more expensive vacations.

Overconsumption, like other drugs, is addictive. Each time we use it, it takes more to fill the void. Each drink or pill or purchase seems to have less effect than the previous one, so we move from a Volkswagen to a Chrysler to a Winnebago; or from a drink before dinner to a drink every hour; or from tobacco to grass to speed.

LOVE

Birth
Blessedness
Blessing
Brothers
Death, dying · John 11:32-36
Poverty · Luke 6:20-21; 21:1-4
Wealth · Mark 12:41-44

Three days ago my brother Randy died.

Two months ago, my first grandchild, Jacob, was born.

Those two events need a lot of meditating on. The holiness and the beauty of those moments are only gradually sinking in. I'm sure I will never understand them fully, if at all.

But the Spirit has been speaking.

Jacob came to us in the poverty of birth. He came weak and naked with nothing but his need. But one day, soon after he was born, I lay down on the sofa with him asleep upon my breast. Jacob sound asleep. Grandpa weeping at the wonder of it all.

Like the widow giving copper coins, unconscious of the greatness of her gift, tiny Jacob gave me love and trust and joy that I will treasure all my life.

And my brother too. There on the hospital bed, the morphine shutting down his eyelids, we spoke to each other from the poverty of his dying and the poverty of my grief. I said words to Randy I had never said before in all the wealthy, healthy 60 years we had been brothers.

"I love you Randy!"

And from the pain-racked poverty of his dying, Randy gave a gift he never could have shared before.

"I love you too," he said.

Blessed are the poor, for they have gifts to give.

LOVE

Commandment
Community
Fathers   John 15:12-14

"Love one another."

That easily ranks as the most popular commandment. And it should be. There is no greater power than love.

Dad was a teacher. He taught high school, and one of the boys in that high school, a classmate of mine actually, was (to be very politically correct) socially challenged. Well, no, that doesn't do it. Stan (not his real name, of course) was royally messed up. He needed help, and he needed it badly.

Stan's dad was chair of the school board, and hence my dad's boss. One day Stan's dad came by our house in that tiny Manitoba town. I was in the shed fixing my bike, so I overheard the conversation he had with my dad who was outside in the garden.

Stan's dad wanted to talk about my dad's chickens, which we kept to supplement the meager teacher's salary. My dad wanted to talk about Stan. Several times, my dad introduced the subject of Stan's problems. Several times, Stan's dad changed the subject to the chickens.

Finally my dad lost his patience. "You are more interested in my chickens than your own son," he blurted out. Stan's dad turned on his heel and left. That night, Dad was called to a special meeting of the school board. He was fired.

When he came home from that meeting, after telling Mom what had happened, he went and wrote a long letter to Stan's dad. Not about being fired. About Stan. "The boy will wind up in jail," said my dad. And he was right. That's exactly where Stan wound up.

Whenever I look for a definition of the kind of practical love Jesus was talking about, I think of my dad's love for Stan.

LOVE
Holiness
Hugs
Image
Sharing   Genesis 1:26-27

I like hugs. I like giving and getting hugs, which is nice because most often you do both at once. The person I hug more than anyone is Bev which is convenient because we're married. It's been quite a while since I've sent her love poems. Come to think of it, I don't think I ever did. She's never asked for any. I think she'd laugh if I sent her one. But she likes hugs.

If we're created in the divine image, maybe that's the divine part. That we need hugs.

Maybe it's the most holy part of us that wants love. Maybe it is the most holy part of us that feels fulfilled when someone shares their love.

MARRIAGE
Cooperation
Housework
Relationships
Teamwork   Romans 8:28

I heard it on the radio. "You can tell whether a married couple is liberated by who makes the bed." Ever since, I've been trying to figure out how knowing who makes the bed tells you that.

Being a naturally sloppy person, I prefer to leave the bed unmade and simply shut the door. It seems logical, since I'm simply going to mess it up again in a few hours.

But if we're going to make it, and Bev insists that we do, then it would seem that the person most capable of making it, should do it. Right? It's only logical.

And Bev, after all, was trained as a young girl to make beds. With a flip and a tug and a pat she can have the whole thing done in no time flat.

I don't manage quite as well. In fact, whenever I flip something, it flips in the wrong direction. If I tug, it pulls out whatever I've tucked in on the other side, and my pats are mostly a desperate last-ditch attempt to flatten the lumps underneath.

So it would seem reasonable that Bev should always make the bed.

However, she seems to feel that since I messed up at least 50% of it, I should straighten out at least 50% of it. And I have to grudgingly admit there is a kind of logic about that.

"OK honey, you make your side, and I'll make mine," I said nobly.

It's a great theory. It doesn't work.

At least not if she makes her side at a different time than I'm making my side, because whoever does it last unmakes the side that was made first. (Do you understand that, or should I run through it again?)

It does work however, if you do it at the same time, and develop a bit of intricate teamwork so that you both tug the sheets just the right amount to pull them tight without yanking them out of the partner's hand. Flip, tug, pat and in about one half of two shakes you can have it done. Actually kind of fun and satisfying.

Maybe real liberation is doing it together.

MARRIAGE

Easter	
Hell	
Hope	
Resurrection	Matthew 28:1-9
Suffering	Luke 24:1-12, 52-53
Weddings	John 20:1-18

In my file of treasured memorabilia, is a photocopied wedding invitation from Margaret Smith and David Gilchrist. No gifts please, because they already have two of everything. Please give a gift to the mission fund of the church.

The invitation reads like this:

"Margaret and Alan Smith settled in Three Hills a decade ago, after serving as a minister in Zambia, Montreal, Saskatoon and Stettler. A couple of years ago, Alan was diagnosed as having Pseudo Bulbar Palsy, which took his life in January, 1990 after eight difficult years of physical but not mental deterioration."

I wept when I read that. Alan was my friend and colleague. His last years were hell, his mind imprisoned in a body that refused to function.

Here's the second half of the invitation.

"David and Margaret Rose Gilchrist moved to Innisfail 13 years ago, after serving churches in Morse, Uranium City and Calgary; and visited the Smiths a couple of times before her cancer was discovered. She suffered for two years before death brought her respite in August, 1989.

"Last fall we decided to accompany each other to a concert and discovered that we had a lot more in common than a love of music and a distaste for loneliness.

"We have both experienced a kind of descent into Hades, and now there is an element of resurrection for us. So Easter seemed an appropriate time to do it. Both the wedding and the supper to follow are open to all. We hope you'll join us."

The resurrection was symbolized by a wedding. Easter Sunday in church, and the groom was the minister. Happy Easter everyone!

MARRIAGE
Family
Humor
Valentine's Day
Weddings   John 2:1-11

Not long ago, Bev did a wedding that made the local newspaper. Not only were both parents of both bride and groom there, but all eight grandparents as well, and all of them still married to each other.

Even just having all four parents still married to each other is unusual these days. As most clergy who do weddings know, figuring out the complex relationships of various parents, stepparents and siblings needs a computer. And the emotions involved in the changing morality defy understanding. A lively sense of humor becomes the minister's most valuable asset.

You've heard the story about the wedding guest who threw a caustic remark to the minister at the reception. "The nerve of the bride wearing white. They've been living together for a year. White is a symbol of virginity."

"Of course," said the minister. "She's what's known as a new revised standard virgin."

Which reminds us of a congregation's annual report that stated, "35 weddings were consummated in the church last year."

The hoary headed among us think fondly of the days when couples got married and then had sex, when marital discord was the exception, and church pews were filled with happy moms and dads, each with 2.5 kids sitting between them.

A little research and common sense tells us those "good ole days" never did exist. As someone said, "nostalgia ain't what it used to be."

The difference now is that we can't ignore it anymore. In our congregation, a couple with three lovely children lit the candles at the beginning of the service. Afterwards, the father told me, "I was thinking, while we were up there, that we're probably the only traditional family left in this congregation."

The Gospel must be good news for all of them – the traditional family and the "revised" virgins. Not necessarily happy news or comfortable news. And it may well be challenging news. But it must be good news.

If the gospel is to be preached, somehow it has to be good news to the grandparents trying to come to terms with changing morality, to the one who lives with verbal or physical abuse, to the recently divorced and the never married, to gays and lesbians, to teenagers wondering where they belong. And to the beautiful family with mom and dad and three kids who come up to light the candle. Platitudes don't work any more, if they ever did. Truth and grace are so hard to articulate. Somehow the sentimentality of Valentine's Day has to be translated into an awareness of God's profligate love expressed in an inclusive community.

MARY MAGDALENE
Disciple
Faithfulness
Jesus   John 13:23, 19:25-26, 21:7

During my study time in Israel, I fell in love with a woman who is not my wife. Bev is not too terribly concerned, however, since the woman in question is Mary of Magdala. Even before the current studies of Gnostic literature by people like Elaine Pagels, we knew she was far more important in the life of Jesus and the early church than the biblical record seemed to indicate.

And I found some tantalizing evidence to that effect, enough to write a paper speculating that she was the mysterious "disciple whom Jesus loved" in John's gospel, and that most certainly she qualified as an apostle, at least using Paul's criteria.

As an exercise, I stripped from John's gospel all the theologizing and sermonizing that got in the way of the narrative. Then I read a very shortened gospel, but one with power and vitality, in which Mary of Magdala was a strong and vigorous character. I'm convinced that much of what I removed had been added by apostolic editors determined to suppress the sensuality of such a woman and any possible hint of a more than platonic relationship with Jesus.

I am not alone in my fascination. Mary of Magdala has been the "virgin-whore" of Christian legend and tradition ever since the early church fathers tried to put the lid on all those rumors, from the "lover" or "wife" or "consort" of Jesus in some Gnostic writings to her evocative "I don't know how to love him" in *Jesus Christ, Superstar*. She's often been confused with the "woman of the city" who washed Jesus' feet with her hair, with Mary of Bethany and even with Mary, the mother of Jesus. Certainly she was with Jesus from early in his ministry in Galilee until the bitter, glorious end – one of the women who kept the whole operation going. She is the only woman in the Bible who is not identified by who "owns" her – husband, father, or brother – but by the town she came from on the shore of Galilee.

Whoever she was, she had suffered greatly and she ministered courageously.

MASCULINITY
Differences
Gender
Healing
Men
Pain
Woundedness   Psalm 147:3

My sister phones me from Winnipeg and thanks me for the book *Man to Man* which came off the press a couple of months back. She wonders how she can get the men in her life to read it. "Why didn't you write that book 20 years ago?" she demands.

Most of the feedback on *Man to Man* has been from women, come to think of it, and it's a troubling thought. Because I wrote the book for men – men who might be scared off by the more heavy-duty male consciousness stuff – dancing and drumming and chanting.

The idea was to provide something that was nonthreatening, entertaining, and yet might open a window or two. And then to provide a fun game to go with it, a game that might generate some discussion on those subjects with other men.

It's way too soon to know if the project has succeeded or failed. But if the women who have spoken to me are any indication, they'll be working on a dozen subtle ways to help make it succeed.

Most of us men hide our wounds with great skill, but we can never escape the pain of them. And very often the demands of the women in our lives, even the very legitimate demands, feed that pain. And we tend to run.

So maybe the time is ripe for a very tender, pastoral sermon directed specifically at men, but one which the women in the pews will be very glad to hear. Such a sermon can probably be preached more easily by women clergy, because we men are too often too self-protective to be able to let others see our wounds. Or even admit to having them. And any good pastoral sermon must begin with the admission of woundedness, and the sharing of pain.

Perhaps if our wounds can be brought into the sunshine of God's love, we men can be healed.

And if we can be healed, then our lives will grow the food that nourishes, rather than sprout the thorns that destroy.

MASS MEDIA

| Manipulation | | Matthew 24:3-5 |
| Seduction | Mark 13:21-23 | Luke 21:7 |

In a waiting room somewhere, I once picked up a magazine that had an article on witchcraft. A phrase jumped out at me. "If you know the words of the incantation, the witch's spell cannot affect you."

I think if we have a little clearer idea of the kinds of stories the mass media are telling us, we'll be a little less likely to be seduced by them.

MASS MEDIA
Consumerism
Entertainment
Information
Journalism
News
Television   Ezekiel 33:1-9

The last few years, I have become increasingly convinced something demonic has invaded the mass media. It's not that the individuals in it are evil (with perhaps a few exceptions). I'd even be prepared to argue that the folks who own the media are not evil. But gradually, over the years, the media industry has moved from a sense of serving people, until now the focus is almost entirely on delivering consumers to the advertisers.

That's problem enough when you consider the content of the endless round of sitcoms and cop shows on TV, mindless patter on radio and vacuous drivel in print. But I am convinced we no longer have any news media in North America. None.

What we have are media that offer reports on events as the content of the entertainment they deliver, in order to attract consumers for their advertisers. The media outlets judge the success of their news "reporting" venture totally on the number of listeners or readers or viewers they can deliver, not on whether it is fair or useful or makes a contribution to democracy.

When the function of a reporter is no longer to report news but to deliver entertaining current events to titillate the consumer, then the news media have become demonic.

MEMBERSHIP
Attendance
Church Attendance
Commitment   Acts 2:44-47

Sometimes I wonder idly what would happen in the congregation where I worship if we prescribed some minimum standards for membership? How about three years of weekly Bible study plus regular church attendance and a regular tithe? 10% off the top. Unless you were willing to make that kind of commitment, you had no right to call yourself Christian, and you could not attend any congregational or board meetings. You could attend church, but you'd never be invited to lead and you would not receive communion.

That would bring the membership in the congregation where I worship down to about a dozen, but they would be a dedicated dozen. They could meet in someone's home and afford to pay a full-time minister, whose salary would be about the average of the member's income. Sounds a little like the New Testament church, doesn't it? Being Christian would really mean something.

No, of course I don't advocate that, but I do wonder about the future of the churches, especially the so-called "mainline" denominations that are going through hard times.

MENNONITES
Community
Story
Theology   Deuteronomy 26:5-8, 6:20

When my Mennonite grandparents settled in the inhospitable west, they found every excuse available to gather together with their neighbors. They told stories and cracked sunflower seeds until the floor was an inch deep in husks. The seeds were high in calories (which they didn't know) and the stories were high in community building (which they felt). It was these stories that helped them know who they were, why they were out there on the cold windy prairie shivering in sod huts, and what their dreams were.

The stories were the fabric that held that Mennonite society together, and communicated to their children and the grandchildren who they were, and what was right and wrong and valuable. In the stories, far more than in the church, they communicated their real understanding of God. It's stories told while eating sunflower seeds that communicate who we really are and what we really believe.

What the preacher says is merely commentary.

METAPHOR
Choice
Healing
Images
Inclusiveness   Matthew 20:1-16
Language   Luke 15:11-32
Perspective   Hosea 11:1-11

There was a man in our congregation for whom the whole communion metaphor was deeply offensive because, he said, it was "liturgical cannibalism." For some, the Father image of God has been offensive. For others the Mother image is. Much depends on our own personal experience of mothers and fathers. Or any image that comes from our experience of human relationships.

I read of one instance where a young woman was raped by her school counselor and now reacts negatively to the line "wonderful counselor, prince of peace." The closer a metaphor or image is to our experience, the more power it has, both positively and negatively.

Recently, in Hanover, Ontario preaching at an anniversary service, I used the metaphor of binocular vision, which humans have and turkeys do not, as a metaphor to show that we can see things from several points of view and therefore add dimension to our vision. After church, an elderly man pointed out that he had lost one eye, and did that make him a turkey? He was laughing, but I wondered if he hurt a little.

One alternative is to be completely objective and clinical about everything we say. No metaphors that might offend. No images that injure. We would be totally inclusive. Or perhaps totally exclusive because we become so clinical and detached that nobody feels particularly included.

The language we have can and should be an instrument of healing. The most healing language is that which touches the soul, that moves the spirit. That kind of language is always made up of rich images and loaded metaphors, the very things that will be most painful to those with deep wounds.

God's grace isn't fair. Or at least it doesn't come in the same way to each of us. I can sit for hours soaking in the rich textures of Mozart. Bev finds Mozart not unpleasant but hardly life-giving. Yet she can stand and stare and soak her spirits in fabric art that I find, well, not unpleasant but hardly life-giving.

I have a friend of many years who is part of the charismatic movement. Praying and speaking in tongues quite clearly fills her with a life-giving spirit that gives her strength to live her faith. Should I deny her that because it means nothing to me?

I find that speaking and writing of a mother God fills me with strength and vitality because I had a particularly strong and life-giving mother. My charismatic friend cannot pray to a mother God because her mother abused then abandoned her. But she affirms my need to pray to a strong and loving mother God.

The parable of the vineyard workers, the parable of the prodigals, the life that Jesus and Hosea and others lived for us, makes it clear to me that God is a profligate lover who cares only that we receive the love.

MISSIONARIES
Call
Evangelism
Ministry
Risk   Genesis 32:22-32

As Jim Taylor tells us, the stories of humans wrestling with God are there in the lives of millions of people who have felt "a hand pushing in the small of the back."

I never felt that hand pushing quite so strongly as the time Bev and I made the decision to "accept the call" to the Philippines as missionaries. There were any number of reasons why that was an unwise move; two tiny children, a career in broadcasting just gaining momentum, no money in the bank and no real understanding of what we were going to and why.

Friends and family advised against it. Some thought we were crazy. We wrestled with God. God won. We went.

Looking back, I realize how much we grew during five years in the Philippines. So in the end, I think we won too.

MISTAKES

Errors
Humor
Metaphors

Sometimes, a few errors creep in.

The folks at Sorrento Anglican Centre in B.C. are noted for their creativity. Sometimes more than others.

For instance, developing an idea from the book *Searching for the Divine Butterfly*, they went one better and advertised a course called "Searching for the Diving Butterfly."

Since Sorrento Centre is right beside beautiful Shuswap Lake, we assume participants were provided with Scuba gear.

We don't know if North Lonsdale United Church is faced with declining Sunday School enrollment. If they are, they certainly tackle the problem with admirable directness. Ann Henning, Sunday School Superintendent, sent around a notice which said, "Our final Church School fathering will take place on May 29th." Ann described it as a "special event."

We'd certainly hope so.

Jim Taylor, in his continuing crusade to save the world from sloppy writing came upon the following: "First, you bite off more than you can chew, but you should learn how to swim before the cows come home to roost."

MISTAKES

Experience
Humor
Learning
Parenthood   Ecclesiastes 2:26b
Preaching   Matthew 13:24-30
Revelation   Genesis 28:16-17

Like every parent, I've preached the little homily to my children, about how it isn't necessary for them to make all the same mistakes I did. "Take my advice and save yourself a lot of trouble." At which point I remember the bit of wisdom that observes that God created parents so teenagers would have something to ignore.

Like every preacher, I have quoted from the pulpit that old aphorism that "those who do not learn the lessons of history are doomed to repeat them." The relationship between preachers and congregations is not unlike that between parents and teenagers.

Then I remember the statement by my friend and colleague, Jim Taylor. He says "God doesn't speak English. Or any other language for that matter. God only speaks through experience."

If that's true, then all my helpful homilies are "vanity and chasing after wind" (Ec 2:26b). There's nothing they can learn from me. The only academic certificate worth having is from the School of Hard Knocks.

At this point an alarm goes off in my head. "Milton, you make a living editing a magazine for preachers (*Aha!!!*), and you are rapidly talking yourself out of a job." To my rescue comes a job-saving insight.

My children are now adults. We can have adult-to-adult conversations. And suddenly I become aware that at least some of my helpful homilies were actually heard and reflected on. *Mirabile Dictu!* They didn't accept what I said as revealed truth by any means, but they used what I said to reflect on their experiences. Sometimes years after the fact, but it happened!

Maybe that's the way it is with congregations too. The pearls of wisdom we cast before them each Sunday are not always trampled into the dirt, but neither are they hung as talismans around their necks. Where our words connect with their experiences, they may reflect. Sometimes years later.

Jim is right. God speaks through experiences. And sometimes the words preachers speak may be the medium God uses to speak through those experiences.

Which may be why God lets both the wheat and the weeds grow side by side in our lives. God wants them both there to speak through. Sometimes the weeds may be as necessary as the wheat. In my own life, it's the weeds God speaks through, though maybe that's because there's far more of them. God would feel a bit limited, I think, having to speak only through the occasional grain of wheat.

I wonder if Jacob would have seen that ladder to heaven, would have been able to hear God there beside him, if his life had not been a tangle of weeds.

MORALITY

Justice	Matthew 5:21
Progress	Exodus 20:13
Social Code	Deuteronomy 5:17

I'm an optimist. I can't help it.

I think we are beginning to learn something in this tired world of ours. We are becoming just a little more mature. There are some good signs along with the troubling signs.

Tribal cultures typically think of morality as applying only to members of the tribe. We experienced that in the rural Philippines where, for instance, it was very wrong to diddle a member of your own clan, but if you could do it to someone outside that circle, well that was fair game.

"Thou shalt not kill," was understood very narrowly by the Hebrews. It applied only to your own clan as did all the rest of the rules.

The idea that the moral and ethical code applied to your whole country grew very gradually during the Reformation, and it even began to include people from other countries. But not other races. Early settlers in Newfoundland hunted aboriginals for sport, and only recently has it dawned on us that not all is fair in love and war. Only after the second world war did the concept of "war crimes" come along, and only in the last few years have we become aware of things like "date rape."

Recently, several Canadian soldiers in Africa on a peacekeeping mission, were charged in connection with the death of a Somali civilian. That wouldn't have occurred to the military a few years ago.

Meanwhile the concept of international law is growing. Slowly and fitfully, but growing. The Canadian military chaplains recently donated money to help the women who had been raped by rampaging soldiers in eastern Europe. The soldiers' freedom to rape used to be considered a legitimate fringe benefit.

And however bumbling the attempts, the fact that the United Nations is taking a hand in the enforcement of human rights, is a move in the right direction.

Our concept of law and justice has grown over the millennia since the Ten Commandments were handed down. Now people of faith are speaking the words from Mount Sinai to the whole world. "Thou shalt not kill."

The killing has not stopped. But for more and more people throughout the world, the killing is seen to be wrong. And that is progress. God's voice is being heard. I believe that someday it will be obeyed.

MOTHERS

Abandonment
Achievement
Death, dying
Pain
Seniors
Useless
Value   Matthew 10:28-31
Worth   Luke 12:6-7

Every father is also a son. For each of us, there comes a time when you find there is no longer someone whose son you can be.

Mother had aged 10 years in 12 months. It's not that there was anything specifically wrong, it's just that everything was wrong.

The fingers that could crochet a pair of slippers in half an hour simply wouldn't move anymore.

The heart that had laughed and cried with all the many people she loved, seemed to have developed some malfunctions. That never stopped her heart from loving, but last Saturday it stopped the heart from beating.

Mother knew death was near. But she wasn't afraid of death. It was the dying that was so painful, so frightening.

Mother and I had a long talk in the hospital a few months ago. She held my hand very tightly and asked, "You won't abandon me just because I'm so useless?"

"Of course not, Mom. How could I abandon you?"

"But I'm so useless. I can't do anything anymore. I'm not good for anything."

"Mom, I love you. Of course I won't abandon you. Neither will the rest of your family."

"But what good am I? I can't do anything except just sit here and stare at the walls."

At first I thought Mother's fear was of being abandoned by her children. But that wasn't it. She knew us better than that. Her pain was far deeper. It was the pain of our whole society that teaches us we are valued for what we can produce, by how well we can perform, by what we can achieve. It was a pain we all share.

Of course, deep down Mother knew the greater truth. Earlier we had been talking about the latest great-grandchild. It had been born on Valentine's day, and we laughed over a photograph showing a heart-shaped birthmark on its bottom.

"I guess babies can't do anything either," she said. I knew what she meant. Babies are useless, but they are precious. Old people are useless, but they are precious. In fact all of us, when you come right down to it, are pretty useless. But we are precious. Precious I hope, to other people. Precious at least to God, who sees the sparrow fall and numbers the hairs on our head.

"Mom," I said. "Do you remember how often you told me about the time when I was just a kid, and I'd be playing out in the back yard, and every once in a while I would run into the house and I would leap up into your arms and get a quick hug, and then run right back out again?" She held my hand a little tighter. She remembered.

"Mom, you had strong arms, and even though I'd take a leap at you, you'd always catch me and give me a hug."

She smiled. "I couldn't catch you in my arms anymore, Ralph."

"I know Mom. But I still come running in for a hug. Only now, you catch me with your heart."

That's why, when we gathered in a church in Winnipeg, all her family and her friends, we didn't gather to mourn, even though there was weeping. We gathered to thank God, and to celebrate the life of a woman who for 82 years was able to catch so many of us in her strong arms and hold us in her loving heart.

MOTHERS

| Fathers | | Matthew 12:46 |
| Parenthood | Luke 8:19 with Mark 3:21 | Mark 3:31-32 |

A mother's love is a focused love. It is not love for the world in general but for one child in particular. That child may be a holy horror, a pugnacious brat, a katzenjammer kid. But the child will be loved by its mother.

Of course I'm romanticizing motherhood. There are rotten, uncaring mothers. There are also gentle caring fathers. And there are people who aren't either, in the biological sense, who are warm, caring, sensitive and have all the other "motherly" virtues. Part of the exclusivism of our culture is that it hangs all this sentimental slush on mothers and it becomes just another way to keep them "in their place." Witness the different connotation of the two terms "mothering" and "fathering."

And as I dodder toward my dotage, and since my mother died some years ago, she can grow unfettered toward her sainthood without much reality standing in the way.

But nevertheless. Even when Mom was in her eighties and I was well into my forties, long married and with four in my own brood, the relationship was never totally adult to adult. When I'd come for a visit, she would give me a warm hug and a kiss, then check to see if I was dressed properly, usually followed by a symbolic straightening of my tie.

And of course, my mother mothered my father. I really have no idea if that caused problems in their relationship. But I have never seen motherly tenderness expressed with such forceful gentleness as the day Mom and I went to see Dad's body in the funeral home. I was the one sobbing. Mom put her arm around my waist, then reached over with her other hand and brushed a wisp of hair away from Dad's forehead.

NAMES

| Heritage | | Genesis 2:20 |
| Pride | Exodus 20:7 | John 14:13, 16:23 |

Mother phoned me long distance to say, "Please don't do it. " I had decided to change my name, and mother felt it was a denial of my family.

I didn't see it that way, at least not then. In show business, you needed a nice clean "English" sounding name. In fact, the radio station manager wouldn't let me use "Friesen" on the air. "Sounds too German!" he said. So I chose one of my given names, and changed "Friesen" to "Milton. " It seemed logical at the time.

Now, a quarter of a century later, I wish I hadn't. But changing back would be even harder. I have a family that bears the Milton name, and a reputation as a writer and speaker where name recognition is important.

But I take increasing pride in the heritage of a people who were bounced around Europe because of their faith. They were followers of Menno Simon, and migrated from Holland to Germany and to Russia.

I still have childhood memories of my grandmother telling stories of how they were pushed out of Russia because of their faith.

It's a noble story, and it's mine. Whatever name I go by.

NEIGHBORS

Community
Relationships   Luke 10:29, 37

As a child, I learned the dialect of the Russian Mennonites. It's a variety of Low German, very similar to Yiddish.

When my family and friends would sit and chat, we had a word for it. Not gossip. Not natter. Not small talk.

The verb is "nobah" which literally translates, "to neighbor." When you sit and talk to each other, just for the sake of talking to each other, you are "neighboring." It's the activity that turns an acquaintance into a neighbor. It's the recognition that small things, the leak in the roof, the child just learning to walk, the state of the garden, the sharing of these small coins of human currency build community.

"Take care of the pounds and the pennies will take care of themselves," is another old saying. Translate that into human relationships, and it means that the little things of life are sometimes more important than the big things. The "insignificant" things we say to our family over breakfast are far more important than the big gifts we may give on a birthday. The casual conversation over coffee in the church hall may be more important than the sermon. The visit over the back fence may be more important than the community meeting.

Which is not to say that we shouldn't give due attention to the large issues that confront us. It is possible to be "penny wise and pound foolish." But it is also true that paying attention to the tiny relationships, the small conversations, is the glue that holds the community together.

So let's import a new word into English, or at least a new use for an old word. When we gather in the fellowship hall after church, when we stand on the street corner and chat, we're not gossiping, we're "neighboring."

We're building community.

OBEDIENCE

Choice
Community
Discipline
Individualism
Liberation   John 14:15-24

We stood at the foot of Mount Sinai, just above the hulking battlement called St. Catherine's Monastery.

Above us, in the arid cliffs, were the remains of caves and huts and tiny dwellings, left by monks who for centuries had prayed their lives away.

"Why?" I wondered. "Why would people spend their lives alone in this desolate place simply praying?"

"Obedience," said my companion. Sister Mary was a nun. She and I and others were here on sabbatical, studying the Bible in the land of the Bible.

"Can't they think for themselves?"

"Of course," said Mary. "Obedience isn't giving up your mind or your freedom. Obedience is choosing, freely, to be guided by the will of God as expressed in a religious community."

For Mary, obedience was a very positive thing. She chose to be obedient to the will of her church and her religious order, because she believes her decisions will be more faithful when made in that community. She chose to accept a discipline, even when sometimes, if it were her decision alone, she might have chosen differently.

"We're so infected with American individualism," Mary said. "For the right wing of the church it's a 'just me and you, Jesus' attitude. For the left wing, it's 'just me and my cause'. "

Sister Mary was convinced that North American Christians involved in social action were using the rhetoric of liberation theology, but really were turn-of-century liberals in disguise. "Because everything is so individualistic. 'If I believe it, it must be right. If I don't believe it, it must be wrong. If that's not my experience, then it's not reality. If it is my experience, then it's the only reality'."

But in liberation theology, liberation comes always to the group, to the community, to the church. There is no such thing as individual liberty, even though "that's what most social justice Christians really believe, when you get beyond the slogans."

That is why, for Sister Mary, liberation meant obedience to her community. Only in obedience could she find liberation.

Which is hard stuff for a Lone Ranger like me to hear.

OPEN-MINDEDNESS

		Acts 10:9-23, 15:1-21
Impartiality	Matthew 15:21-28	Mark 7:24-30

I'm trying to make a case for disciplined openness. Reuel Howe calls it "the principle of dialogue"; genuine sharing and genuine listening. It is the opposite of faithfully reading only those materials that support your point of view, relating only to people who think and act as you do, and generally avoiding the possibility that you might discover a better truth than the one you've been holding on to.

PEACE
Future
Refreshment
Trust
Worry   Luke 2: 25-35

Last summer, Bev and I camped for a week near the village of Plains in Washington State on the campus of the Grünewald Guild, of which the noted artist, Richard Caemmerer, Jr. is the guru.

His tradition is Lutheran, and so each evening we used the Compline service as our vespers, which included Simeon's ancient song, "Lord, now let thy servant depart in peace, according to thy word..."

I didn't like it the first couple of evenings. After all, that is Simeon saying he is ready to die. His life is complete.

Well mine isn't. I have a whole string of things I still want to do, and I go to bed with my head buzzing with all the stuff I'm going to do tomorrow. Or else, I lie there worrying about somebody, my children, my friends, my wife, myself – there's no shortage of folks to worry about. Or I worry about my work or the world situation –

there's no shortage of issues to worry about.

But one night at Grünewald, I found myself lying there in bed with Simeon's song singing in my head. I let the song do its work, and I drifted off quickly into a quiet sleep and woke up the next morning refreshed.

The future of the world is not in my hands. It is in God's hands, and God has done what is needed. God has sent the Christ to be with us. We can depart – to sleep or to a new phase of our life, to death – in peace.

PERCEPTION

Action Attentiveness
Awareness   Matthew 13:14   Mark 4:12
Photography   Acts 28:26-28   Isaiah 6:9

If I claimed to be an athlete, it would stretch your credibility and mine to the point of breaking. But I do have one attribute in common with many famous athletes. I have excellent peripheral vision.

Wayne Gretzky, "the great one," is (or was) probably hockey's greatest player. One of his skills is the ability to anticipate where the play is moving, and to do that, he relies on an amazing peripheral vision. "He's got eyes in his ears," the sports commentators crow. His "greatness" has everything to do with his ability to see what is happening, to notice what's going on especially around the edges.

I am a better photographer than I am an athlete – which is not saying much. My photography hero is Freeman Patterson, a theologically trained photographer who produced an amazing book called, *Photography and the Art of Seeing*.

Many years ago I took a night-school course in photography. One of our tasks was "to learn to really see the pictures." We were given three rolls of film and told to go to a very familiar place in our home, "a room you go into every day," and take three rolls of pictures.

I'm not sure why I chose to do this in the bathroom, but it took several hours of looking through the viewfinder at taps and toilet rolls before I completed my assignment.

"What's Dad doing in the bathroom?" the children asked Bev.

"He's taking pictures," was her somewhat strained response.

"Of what?"

I couldn't hear the response, and I was just as glad. But the exercise did demonstrate Freeman Patterson's thesis – that real photography is only slightly related to the technical aspects of camera operation, and everything to do with the ability to see. To notice. Especially to notice what's around the edges as well as in the middle.

Photography is a lot like sermon preparation.

My colleague Jim Taylor does much the same thing at the spiritual level. In sermons and workshops and conversation he urges people to pay attention – to look closely and carefully – at what is happening to them, because if you look at life through the viewfinder of faith, you get a picture of God in action.

PERSEVERANCE
Dedication
Impulsiveness
Risk
The Whole People of God (curriculum)

One of the most exciting stories in my life becomes a reflection on the need for impulsive risk taking and steadfast dedication.

A number of years ago, a group of Christian people in the small city of Regina, Saskatchewan made the utterly idiotic, impulsive, impractical decision to write their own church school curriculum. None of them had any idea what was involved. It was a courageous and silly thing to undertake.

They had something else besides courage. They had, what my Dad used to call, "stick-to-it-iveness." They worked morning, noon and night for years. And by golly, they wrote a dandy curriculum called *The Whole People of God*.

After getting the cold shoulder from their denominational headquarters, the Regina folk approached our small publishing company called Wood Lake Books. We made the utterly ludicrous decision to publish it. It could so easily have sunk us, and several times it came within a whisper of doing just that.

But the project attracted a group of people who worked morning, noon and night to get that curriculum published. They're still at it, years later, working steadily day in and day out, often putting in long hours of overtime. And that curriculum is now being used by thousands of congregations. It's published in five different editions in three countries.

Without the impulsive decisions, it wouldn't have happened.

Without the dedicated, day by day hard work, it wouldn't have happened.

God needs all kinds of gifts. Impulsive lavishness. And the steadfast caution of those who simply keep at it, day after day.

PORNOGRAPHY

Personalities	Matthew 19:5
Relationships	Mark 10:8
Sex	Genesis 2:24

Madonna (the pop singer) may be an expert on sex, but I wonder what she knows about making love. "Making love" is not a very helpful euphemism for sex.

The tragedy of the porno plague is not the display of nudity or even public copulation. The tragedy lies in the poverty of the relationships, the poverty of the personalities involved, the poverty of the act.

PORNOGRAPHY

Honesty
Sex
Truth   Philippians 4:8

There's a bookstore in the town of Banff that deserves a small award for "telling it like it is." Over each section in the store is a nicely carved-in-wood sign identifying the category of reading material found there.

Over to the side is a section labeled very simply, "Smut."

PRAYER

Spirituality
                                                         Matthew 6:9

The method of prayer that works for me is to think of something that happened in the last week or so. I tell that story to God, in words that form in my head. I try to say what I did, what others did, and how I feel. I express myself in the kind of language I normally use. Sometimes this includes some old-fashioned four-letter words. I don't think God minds.

After I've told God everything, I try to listen. That's called praying.

PREACHING
Conservatism
Evangelical
Homiletics
Prayer   Jeremiah 5:14-15, 8:10-11

This one comes from a Toronto cleric who insisted he not be identified.

It seems a young minister was very discouraged, after trying to preach a few sermons about issues of justice and peace.

"The people here prefer Jesus Weejis preaching," a fellow minister told the young man. He didn't know what "Jesus Weejis" meant. He wondered if that was covered at College the week he had the flu. Finally, he got up enough courage to ask what "Jesus Weejis" preaching meant.

"Oh," said the other. "They want to hear things like, 'Jesus we jis want to say thank you' and 'Jesus, we jis want to love you'."

PREACHING
Communication
Homiletics   Isaiah 6:9-10
Sermons   Any of the many references
Understanding   to hearing and (not) understanding

My wife is a preacher. "Did you know, Bev," I said, "that communication theory and research indicates preaching is a viable form of communication?" She gave me a look that said very clearly "You're full of bologna."

She might also have been tempted to quote the 33rd chapter of Ezekiel at me: "They keep saying, 'Come and hear the word that has come from Yahweh'. They throng towards you; my people sit down in front of you and listen to your words, but they do not act on them."

Or she might have read me the sixth chapter of Isaiah, where God is quoted as saying, "You may listen and listen, but you will not understand. You may look and look again, but you will never know."

Like most clergy, Bev isn't really convinced that sermons are particularly effective. Like most lay people, I'm convinced that a good sermon well-preached can be very effective.

According to Reuel Howe, a survey he did indicates that 80% of the lay people thought the sermon was the most meaningful part of the service. He didn't say what the rest thought.

Rod Booth was sitting at his desk, shaking his head. He was the minister at the church I attended almost two decades ago. Rod is the kind of person who goes out on a limb, even when he hears the sound of sawing. This time he looked as if he could hear the wood cracking.

"Look at this," he moaned. "I asked fifteen people in the congregation to write in one paragraph what they thought was the main point in the sermon. Want to know what they said?"

"Sure!"

Rod threw the batch of papers up in the air. "Every one of them said something different," he said. "only two of them came close to what I thought I was saying."

Reuel Howe had the same results in his studies. Less than a third of the pew-sitters he surveyed knew what the preacher was talking about. That should sound devastating.

It's no wonder Bev gave me that look when I said preaching was a viable form of communication. Obviously, I have some explaining to do.

PREACHING
Homiletics
Sermons

S. J. Wylie was an intrepid Irishman who has preached sermons on three continents in a style that probably died with him. He may have been the last of the great orators.

"You know what I dislike most?" This was after a preaching tour of Australia. "It's all those faces sliding by saying, 'I enjoyed your sermon.' Poppycock!"

A week later he bounced up to me to describe a fine five-point sermon he had preached. He was delighted at a gray haired lady, who took his hand on her way out of church, looked him square in the eye and said, "I can't stand your guff! "

PREACHING

Audience
Clergy
Communication
Community
Education
Entertainment
Homiletics
Words

"Promiscuous! How can preaching be promiscuous?"

An understandable reaction. I had just given my standard answer to the question, "Do you get invited to preach very often?"

"Yes," I said. "I preach around quite a bit."

"That sounds vaguely promiscuous."

"It is."

I've always understood preaching as an intimate act between pastor and the gathered community. Preaching at its best happens when the preaching springs out of the life, the hurting, the joy, the passion of the community. It's almost in the category of pillow talk.

I don't feel good about preaching except in my own home congregation. In other congregations, I go in, have my say and leave. That's it. I don't know who they are. They don't know who I am. And I'm not there afterwards to pick up the pieces.

Do I enjoy it? Of course I do. And the feedback I get from the congregations where I preach is that they like it too. I can whomp out a pretty good speech.

But when they discreetly hand me an envelope with a cheque in it, I wonder if there's a bit of a gigolo in me. I get my jollies. They get their strokes. I take my money and leave. Wham! Bam! Thank you Ma'am.

Of course that's overstating the case. It's like a whack on the head. It gets attention. It helps us focus.

Every theology of preaching I've ever read has said that preaching is not entertainment and it's not education. Preaching is not a sacrament, but it is sacramental in that through it the Word may happen. When a sermon is faithfully preached and faithfully heard, there is the Gospel.

I'm not convinced that happens when I go into a strange church and do my thing. To some degree, the same problem is there when

I visit other churches. When I'm traveling, I visit lots of different churches and I've heard sermons that were mostly entertainment, or mostly education.

Some are almost caricatures. High profile preacher. Lots of piz-zazz. Lots of jokes. Lively, entertaining sermon. "You gotta come and hear our Rev," the folks are saying. "Really good!" So people come and "hear the Rev." The best two-buck show in town. Those churches are full on Sundays. But the people in the pews are an audience, not a congregation.

The other extreme. Sermons are well-researched, reflecting the latest relevant social concerns. Every point is tightly argued. A few in the congregations find this very helpful. Most shut off their minds. The sermon dies on the steps of the chancel. It's all good, worth-while stuff but it gets nowhere.

On the other hand, I have worshiped in congregations where I felt like a guest in someone else's home. That's exactly as it should be. There were in-jokes and references and history and relation-ships I didn't understand. The sermon was not designed to impress me. I was welcome to listen but the preacher was in conversation with the community. The sermon sprang out of a deep and caring relationship. On many of the faces I could see deep participation.

I recognize this and warm to it. I know it from my home congre-gation. A community confronting the Gospel together.

PREACHING
Clergy
Homiletics
Preparation
Sermons

Most preachers, it seems to me, have enough biblical background or at least the resources to find whatever information they need. But they often don't ask the primary preaching questions: "Where does my own life intersect with this? "What do I feel about this?" "What can I, personally, say with conviction about this?" "Where are the people I'm going to preach to on this subject? How do they feel about it?"

Preachers who begin sermon preparation by reading commen-taries seldom get around to those essential questions – the ones that give passion and conviction to a sermon. I feel quite strongly that scholarly, analytical and other materials are important but secondary resources for sermon preparation. The primary resource is the life and work and people of the worshiping community interacting with the biblical witness. That's good communication theory, basic liberation theology and solid pedagogy. Pastor/preachers helping preacher/pastors to preach.

PREACHING
Clergy
Homiletics
Sermons

Where does the preacher start? From the needs of the congregation? The imperative of the text? Traditional homiletics insists it must be the imperative of the text (isn't that the fundamental point of the lectionary, after all?), but like other laypeople, I've never studied homiletics (traditional or otherwise) and so I simply come to church hoping the preacher will speak to my need.

Most preachers (myself included when I do it) don't do either. We speak from our own needs. Few of us realize or admit that. But it's not a bad thing. When my own minister speaks from his own needs, from his own fears and confusions, he speaks to mine as well.

PREJUDICE
Attitude
Charismatic
Differences
Openness   Acts 10:9-29

Two years ago I went to Lethbridge to film a program segment with a charismatic prayer group. I went with a knot in my stomach and my head full of thoughts about "kooky charismatics" who speak a strange gibberish and are generally just plain weird. I gave myself a little talking-to, swallowed hard, and went in there with as much of an open mind as I could manage.

That little bit of openness, that small attempt to set aside my preconceived notions, was enough to result in an open and warm encounter. Soon I found myself in deep discussion and sharing; and I discovered some warm and caring friends.

PREJUDICE

Immigrants
War   Matthew 5:43-48, especially v.45

Dad was fluently trilingual. English, German, and the "low-German" of the Russian Mennonites.

So during W.W.II, Dad worked with the censorship department of the armed forces, checking mail between a group of German prisoners incarcerated in Canada and their families in Europe.

The job wasn't all that hard. The pay was good. During the three years he did the job, Dad didn't find a thing in any of the mail that could be called "sensitive information." But he did begin to see the war through different eyes.

During the war, Germans and Japanese were portrayed in the north American media as power-mad maniacs out to conquer the world and destroy civilization. But Dad couldn't find those kinds of Germans in the mail he was reading. "They're ordinary people, just like us, and they are just as confused and upset about what is going on as we are."

Dad was technically in the military. He could have been court-marshaled for some of the things he told his kids. He could have been thrown in the slammer for bringing home some beautifully etched artwork a mother had sent to Hans, her son in prison. All artwork was suspect and to be destroyed, said the rules, but Dad slipped it in his pocket and brought it home to show us. It was exquisite and tender. After the war Dad located Hans in Germany and sent him the card. His mother had disappeared in the war. Hans had no other mementos.

Dad helped me see through different eyes. As a boy I learned that in any conflict, good is never only on one side. Nor evil. Dad looked past the caricature of fear and saw a child of God.

RACE
Civil Rights
Consciousness
Feminism
Men's Movement   1 Corinthians 11:1-16, 14:33b-36
Radicalism   Ephesians 5:22-24

I attended school in the back seat of a Chrysler sedan for five years.

Working in New York, living in New Jersey, I was part of a car pool going back and forth each day. We lived in a black neighborhood. I was the only white in that car. The others were, to a person, involved in the black liberation movement which was then at its height, with Martin Luther King preaching the gospel of liberation loudly and clearly.

This was in the '60s. Like most white Canadians, I lived with the fiction that Canadians didn't have a race problem. Often I would think it, and occasionally I would say it. "Look, I am a Canadian. What's happening here is not my fault. Why are you dumping on me?"

It's taken me a couple of decades to understand why.

I'm involved in the men's movement a fair bit. One of the discussions that happens over and over is men saying, "Look, I treat women as equals. Why are they mad at me?" Sometimes we give ourselves away by saying things like, "I've always given the little woman everything she asked for." One of the hardest things to get men to realize is that all of us have an investment in the hierarchical assumptions and the structures that give rise to the Marc Lepines, who go and massacre women. Our culture provides the soil in which such monsters, and many lesser monsters grow.

RADICALISM
Activism
John the Baptist
Justice
Power   Matthew 3:7, 14:1-12
Revolution   Mark 6:17-29
Techniques   Luke 3:7-14

In the news today, a story about the Greenpeace people staging a sit-in at the French Consulate in Vancouver. They were protesting nuclear tests in the South Pacific.

Is it too much of a stretch to say that Greenpeace is the modern equivalent of John the Baptist?

Those of us who cut our political and religious eye teeth in the '60s. have moved into the suburbs with the rest of the hippies and learned how to mow lawns and barbecue. And to us, the activities of the Greenpeacers seems a bit – well – melodramatic. In fact, a goodly number of us wonder whether a democracy can survive when governments seem to respond mostly to special interest groups on both the left and the right.

What is the role of the radical fringe? Do we need the extremists who chain themselves to trees and paint baby seals green and ram their boat into other vessels? Maybe they focus our attention and make the more moderate voices sound most reasonable and conciliatory. Could Martin Luther King have succeeded without Macolm X? Did the rantings of John the Baptist make Jesus sound reasonable and subdued? At least for the first year or so of his ministry?

Marcus Borg and others say Jesus was a disciple of John. If that's the case, Jesus may have left the movement, not because he disagreed, but because John was a little too – well melodramatic. But Jesus may have been able to plant good seed because John stirred up the soil.

Now I find myself worried. In my own denomination – for that matter in any of the ecumenical mainline denominations in North America – there don't seem to be any John the Baptists kicking up a fuss with outrageous statements and weird, controversial tactics. Yes, we have the same liberal-conservative split that every mainline denomination has, but nobody at either extreme is making any blood boil. There's nobody, at least as far as I know, who we would admit to being "one of us," who is sending church leadership into special meetings. Nobody over whom we suck air through our teeth and say, "What has this person done (or said) this time?"

Without such a person, are those of us who are of a more moderate bent, essentially powerless?

RECOVENANTING
Attendance
Congregations
Covenant
Faith
Family

1 Corinthians 12

A rap for Recovenanting Sunday

> Hey look! All of us are gathered here
> Lookin' sorta' fresh and full of cheer.
> Why do you think we've gotten together?
> A change of heart? Or a change in the weather?
>
> The kids are gettin' ready to start their classes.
> You're good lookin' lads and fine lookin' lasses.
> You're going to learn to live in God's way.
> It won't be easy, but that's OK.
>
> Some are lookin' tanned and some pretty tired.
> Some are bored stiff and some are kinda wired.
> We've come here looking for goodness knows what!
> Preaching that's cool? Singing that's hot?
>
> We're looking for meaning. We're looking for life!
> To make some sense out of trouble and strife.
> Something is missing in our lives for sure.
> The preacher hasn't got the sure-fire cure.
>
> Well here's the news I've come to tell!
> All of us together can make you feel well.
> You'll discover, if you join us here,
> That we pull together to work through fear.
>
> Give your heart to a loving God,
> You'll find a truth profound and odd.
> God will love you through friends at your side.
> As you work together, you'll be satisfied.
>
> You don't have to sit all alone in a pew.
> Lean on us and we'll lean on you.
> We'll work and struggle; we'll sing and pray –
> All together, we're God's family.

RESOLUTIONS

Failure
Grace
Guilte
New Year   Philippians 4:7

For reasons that are much too boring to mention, I am on a zillion mailing lists. Some of those are lists aimed at "business people."

And so I get a bundle of advertising every day, and almost always there is something promoting another seminar, or another computer program, or some new gimmick to help me plan my time effectively so that I can "maximize" my efficiency and churn out more work more effectively and more profitably.

I have paid big bucks to attend those seminars, and I have bought those programs, made diligent notes, read all the literature and come home full of good intentions. They never last, and all I'm left with is a sense of failure.

Every New Year I clean up my office, organize my calendar, straighten out my files and try to be much more responsive to the needs of others. Two or three days later it's as chaotic as ever, and I'm feeling guilty. You see, I have no problem making good resolutions. I just can't keep them.

I know all the theories, all the rhetoric about self-discipline. I just don't have any. And if I try harder to develop some, all I get is a dose of the guilts.

The only reason my life has some semblance of sanity is because there are good, kind, generous people around who help me.

This New Year I've resolved not to make any resolutions except one I think I might be able to keep. I will be consciously thankful for the wonderful grace I receive. I'll be as dysfunctional as ever about many aspects of my life, but I will know that God's angels, angels with names like Bev and Cynthia and Joanne and Jim and Norah and Kari care about me and will continue to help me make something beautiful out of my madly chaotic life.

REWARD

Children
Faith
Hope
Music
Patience   Matthew 10:40-42
Teachers   Luke 6

Want to know how I got my bald spot? Or why I have this nervous twitch? Music!

The first time it happened I was walking down the hallway of a junior college. There, in one of the rooms, was a music teacher, a woman about eight feet tall in both directions. Beside her was a child no more than two feet high.

In her sweaty little hand the child had one of those Suzuki violins, about six inches long. From that small instrument she produced a squeal that loosened my dandruff and cured my fallen arches. It took three visits to the dentist to re-seat my back teeth.

But the teacher, bless her, smiled very nicely and said, "That was lovely, Susy. Now try again, but this time don't press quite so hard."

I panicked. I ran the hundred yard dash in twelve seconds flat, enough to get out of earshot, but by then I had a slight curvature of the spine and my hair was falling out.

The rest of my hair fell when my own son started learning the violin. Did you know that the sound of a violin, when played just slightly sharp, can penetrate even the dark recesses of a bathroom when the water's running? And when a second son started on the trumpet, an instrument capable of bringing water to a boil long before the microwave was invented, I developed a nervous twitch.

All of this brings me to a very important theological issue. It seems to me, if there is any justice in the life hereafter, surely Susy's teacher and my kids' music instructors and all their long-suffering colleagues should have some special heavenly reward. They get precious little down here.

So, in case God is interested, I'd like to suggest a room in that celestial palace where clean, well washed polite cherubs who never chew bubble gum will arrive on time and well practiced for all their lessons. And they will play everything perfectly in tune.

And while I'm at it, may I humbly suggest a room be reserved for us parents of music students. Hopefully in doing so, the good Lord will overlook a few unkind words and temper tantrums, considering all we've been through.

The executive suite in that pearly palace should be reserved, I'm convinced, for people like Mrs. McNish. Mrs. McNish teaches band in a junior high school; four classes of grade seven students. In each class there are forty students. Do you have any idea, any concept, of what a grade seven student sounds like the first time he or she blows a trombone? Well, it's somewhere between the sound of an asthmatic diesel locomotive and a water buffalo with hemorrhoids.

Multiply that by forty, continue for thirty minutes and repeat four times daily. It's the fastest prescription available for turning a good mind into Silly Putty.

Mrs. McNish is either a person of fantastic faith or utmost imbecility. She believes, yes believes, that one day those drippy-nosed grade sevens blasting that mind-bending cacophony, those pubescent preteens blowing peanut butter particles into their piccolos, will one day take a chair in a great orchestra – the Berlin Symphony or even Lawrence Welk.

Music teachers of the world – there is good news! Luke, Chapter 6. "Blessed are those who weep, for they shall laugh."

RISK
Children
Exploration
Parenting
Worry   Luke 19:4

A few years ago, when my kids were small, I sat in the back yard of our home in Teaneck, NJ, watching them climb all over a gnarled old apple tree. My knuckles were white, my stomach was in a knot. I wanted so badly to go and help them; to hold them so they wouldn't fall. I didn't. I just sat there and worried. I knew they had to learn to climb on their own, to explore their abilities. Taking risks is the price of growing up.

Now that they are older, I can share that story with them, along with a lot of other stories about their childhood and mine.

I know they may laugh at me (they often do!) or that they may think less of me because of what I reveal. I'll risk that. Even on the ripe side of sixty, risking is still the price of growing.

RITUAL

Baptism
Ceremony
Confirmation
Weddings

In ritual, we act out our faith, we create a drama that says to us and others: "This we believe even though we can't tell you why. "This is important!"

I really regret the loss of ceremony in many of our church traditions, because the loss robs us of a sense of "occasion." In the process of ridding ourselves of calcified meaningless ritual, we lost our sense of marking occasions in such a way as to burn them into our beings with their significance.

Infant baptism ceremonies are often very disappointing to me. Baptisms apparently take too much time so we line them up and run them through. That assembly-line processing has a message far louder than the words the pastor uses, words which speak of the significance of the vows the parents and the congregation take. Then we wonder why people don't take baptism seriously, why they phone the church at the last minute to have their kids "done."

That may also be one of the reasons why marriage isn't taken as seriously as it once was. I'm certainly not suggesting this is a central reason, but I do feel it's a factor. We run through them, 20 minutes; "next please"; six or seven in an afternoon in some churches.

Baptisms, weddings and all other events should be marked as "occasions." We should make a fuss over them, with elaborate preparations and arguments over what to wear. There should be pomp and circumstance and singing. If it takes time away from the sermon, we may need to realize that what we do is also a sermon.

The little drama we enact in the baptism, wedding, confirmation or whatever, is a wordless sermon that says, "Mark this!"

SALVATION

Harry   Step right up folks, salvation in a bottle. Save your eternal soul. $9.99, plus tax of course.

Larry   What do you mean? You can't save my soul for $9.99. You can't sell God's grace in a bottle.

Harry   Of course I can. What is God's grace except feeling good. When you're feeling good, you know God likes you. When you're not feeling good, you know God hates you. For $9.99 my bottled salvation will keep you feeling good.

Larry   You mean I don't have to do anything. No loving my neighbor? No giving to help the poor? No caring for justice?

Harry   Justice, shmustice. You look after yourself, let the others look after themselves. Salvation is just between you and God. God helps those who help themselves. Take home a bottle of salvation, you'll feel good about everything, you'll be set for this life.

Larry   What about the next life?

Harry   No problem. Harry's bottled salvation will grease the skids right into heaven for you. If you feel good here, you're bound to feel good in the hereafter.

Larry   Do you take credit cards?

Harry   Absolutely. Feel good now, pray later.

SERMONS

A lady asked my friend, Harold Alston, after one of his sermons, "Do you preach the whole Gospel?"

"Not every Sunday," was his reply.

SPIRITUAL GROWTH

Faith
Relevance
Tolerance
Trinity
Truth   Matthew 28:19

My, how we like to have things nailed down.

During a session in a Marriage Encounter weekend, I got quite irritated at Bev because she refused to be pinned down about exactly how she felt on certain issues.

Because I seldom have helpful insights at the moment I need them, I "harrumphed" at her refusal to be specific and changed the subject. It's in retrospect that I sometimes understand things a bit better, and that's when I realized my demand was both unrealistic and silly.

Bev is a living human being, and a living thing is by definition a changing thing. She can't say anything that will be true for all time, and neither can I. We are all complex, changing people, and what we are today is not what we were yesterday and not what we will be tomorrow. That includes the way we think about things.

Our faith is our interaction with God. God's being is expressed through our ever changing lives. There is no objective "truth" out there which we could articulate even if we were clever enough to remove all the encrustations of culture and personality. We are, as the early church was, "people of the Way," and we can only put words around the reality we perceive at this particular point on our journey. And we don't do that terribly well either.

The Trinitarian formula was useful to the early church as it is useful to us now, but we understand it differently because we are a different people living in a different time and culture, expressing ourselves in a very different language. We think differently because we are different.

Let's stop fussing over who is "right" or "wrong." Let's stop fussing about who is using the "historically correct" or the "liturgically correct" or the "politically correct" formula. At best, it's an arrogant exercise.

Let's hold up the light we have, and appreciate the light that others have. Both will illuminate our path, if we let them. We are called to journey in faithfulness, to "walk the mile and share the load."

God will decide who is right and who is wrong. Although I have a strange feeling God doesn't particularly care.

STORY
Imagination
Perspective
Sharing
Trust

When I was a child, my father told us stories about Pete and Nete. He made them up in his head. Pete and Nete had brown cookies and white cookies. The brown cookies made them grow larger, the white cookies made them grow smaller. Around that Dad built all sorts of adventures.

Dad usually told the stories just before bed. I can remember lying there in my room, thinking about Pete and Nete, imagining myself in their places, decorating my father's sparse plots with the colors of my boyish imagination.

I knew a lot more about Pete and Nete than my Father did, and I'm not sure he would have approved of all the adventures those two mythical boys had in my head. Like the time we stole a locomotive so we could "get to Winnipeg fast."

When you can tell me your story, and I can bring to it my own feelings, my own past, my own peculiar way of seeing things, then your story can speak to where I live. I may change it around a bit in the process.

If you can accept my doing that, then your story becomes a precious gift to me, and I make it truly my own. Sharing a story is an act of trust.

STORYTELLING
Folklore

A very old legend:

When the Baal Shem had a very hard task to do, he'd go to a very special place in the woods where he would light a fire and pray. And whatever the task was, it was done.

A generation later, the Maggid of Meseritz had the same hard task to do. He went to the same place in the woods where he said,

"We can no longer light the fire, but we can still say the prayers." Again, the task was done.

Another generation passed and Rabbi Moshe Leib of Sassov had to perform this task. The good Rabbi went into the woods and said, "We can no longer light the fire. And we don't remember the words for the prayers. But we do remember this special place in the woods where it all belongs, and that must be sufficient. " It was.

But then another generation passed. Rabbi Israel of Rishin found himself faced with that difficult task. He sat down on his chair and said, "We cannot light the fire. We do not know the words for the prayers, and we have forgotten the way to the place in the woods. But we can tell the story of how it was done."

Once more, the task was done!

SUFFERING

Consolation
Experience
Healing
Insight
Love
Pain
Parent
Parenting   Psalm 139
Strength   Matthew 28:20

Like every father, I had my children fooled for awhile. Until they were about two or three. Up till then, they were convinced their dad could fix anything. And dad usually could. But alas, babies grow up and discover that papa is not omnipotent – that papa cannot fix all the broken toys, much less the broken dreams and relationships, and that when he kisses it better, the pain doesn't always stop.

Early in my journey of faith, I looked toward God much as a two-year-old looks toward a parent. I came running to God with whatever was broken in my life, and for awhile it seemed as if God fixed things. Then I realized that God didn't really, or couldn't really. God was, and is still, willing to kiss the place in me that hurts, but that doesn't make the pain go away. It still hurts, but God's love helps me handle it.

As my children got older, I would sit and hold them till the crying stopped and the hurt became bearable. I would carry them on my shoulders until the sore toe was healed enough so they could walk again. And when they had an argument with a friend or a problem at school, we would talk about it together, and sometimes we could find a way for the hurt to be healed.

It's dangerous using human analogies to understand God, but I don't think there's a better way. Abstract definitions and descriptions don't help a bit. God is the God we experience through lives that touch ours – through people we experience – the communion of saints that we've known personally or read about in the scripture and elsewhere. In my life, those saints have offered no cures for anything, but they have sometimes made healing possible.

My reading of the Bible, my sense of history, is that God doesn't like the "Mr. Fixit" role very much, though I have no doubt God can and does act in that way sometimes. God seems to lurk, constantly, just on the edge of our consciousness, ready to offer consolation, insight, strength, memory, warmth, love, when we are willing to receive it. And this is true for systems and organizations and governments, as well as for individuals. God is always there to offer healing.

SUFFERING

Blessing	
Hurt	
Pain	Passion narratives
Story	2 Corinthians 1:3-7

The Hi and Lois cartoon had the teenager, the eldest of the two sons wailing away to his guitar. The younger brother asks, "That's neat. Can you teach me to sing like that?"

Teenage brother says, "You can't sing like that until you've really suffered."

The next frame has little brother in dark glasses walking around moaning and groaning. "What's the matter with him?" asks Hi. "I don't know," says Lois. "He was quite cheerful this morning."

If there's a moral to that story, it's that suffering is relative. An ingrown toenail is hardly the stuff of great tragic drama, unless you're half-way through a long hike and the thing starts hurting. No suffering preoccupies us more than our suffering.

The great cosmic question addressed by most religions in one

way or another is not, "What is the meaning of life?" Or any varia-
tions on that. The central religious question for most of humankind
is: "Why does it have to hurt?" Or as old Tevya said in *Fiddler on the
Roof*, "God, is this really necessary?"

And because there are few answers forthcoming from anywhere,
or at least few answers that seem to make any sense or do any good,
we do our best to run and hide from suffering. Is there anything
more natural, more understandable than that?

But those of us with the theological disease like to call on people
to "enter into the suffering." I have often told, with smug self-
righteousness, the story of the congregation who ordered their
preacher to move directly from Palm Sunday to Easter morning
to avoid all the messiness in-between. Yet I know, if it was my
own personal pain I was going through during Passion week, not
the pain of a man 2,000 years ago, I would high tail it to my neighborhood sawbones looking for a good strong narcotic.

And yet, we see the glowing lives of some who have suffered greatly
and been deeply blessed through that suffering. At the same time we
see the shattered remains of those who have been destroyed by it.

Maybe the problem is that we try to explain things. Maybe the
early church had the right idea (which Paul never quite understood) that the best thing is to tell the story. And the stories. Again,
and again and again.

Explain it, and we get the only reasonable response: "Suffering?
Redemptive? Gimme a break!"

SUFFERING
Beauty
Healing
Hope
Pain   Romans 8:18

I met a woman the other day. Her face was lined and etched and
wrinkled by a life of pain most of us can only half imagine. But as I
looked at her face, I saw a noble, lustrous beauty there that I'll not
soon forget.

Her face is a pearl. A pearl is a wound, a wound that has healed
into something beautiful.

When a grain of sand or something foreign gets into an oyster
shell, the nacre, the inner shell of the oyster forms coating after

coating of a beautiful lustrous substance around the object. The pearl is the healing of a wound to protect the soft body of the oyster, but we discover an object of great beauty formed in that oyster's pain.

SUPPORT

Experiencing God
Fathers
Fear
Help
Nurture
Past Experience   Christmas narratives
Punishment   John 3:16-17

"Don't try to play God!"

Throw that into any discussion and it becomes an almost unanswerable statement.

But perhaps that's exactly what God wants us to do.

I played God a couple of years ago because I happened to be in the right place at the wrong time. Or perhaps the right time. I was shanghaied by a church school teacher at the top of the basement stairs.

"I need your help. Now!" she said, and led me by the arm into one of the Sunday School rooms. The problem was obvious. Young Peter was dressed as a shepherd for the Christmas pageant, and he was using his shepherd's staff to hold the entire class at bay. He was swinging it around while the rest of the class cowered in a corner.

"Give me that stick!" I said to Peter from well out of range.

"Go to hell!" said Peter.

I walked closer. Peter swung the staff at me, I caught it in my hand, and yes it hurt. But I hung on and so did Peter. I pulled him toward me and threw both my arms around him. And I held him in a bear-hug while he struggled.

He struggled long and hard and shouted all sorts of profanity at me. I simply hung on, my arms wrapped around him. Eventually his struggling and his curses dissolved into tears. He released his hold on the staff, and gradually the bear-hug turned into a human hug.

"You're going to beat the pants off me, aren't you?" Peter finally asked.

"Why would I do that?"

"Because that's what my dad always does."

"Does he do that often."

"Yeah. He comes home drunk all the time and beats me and my mom and everybody except the baby."

"I don't want to beat you, Peter. I want to be your friend."

"Nobody wants to be my friend. Whenever I get a friend I hit them and then we're not friends anymore." Peter began to cry again. By this time he was sitting on my lap, my arms still around him, but making no attempt to leave. I wondered if this was the first time he'd ever been cuddled by a man. Did he know that men can love as well as hurt?

"Are they going to kick me out of the church play?" Peter asked.

"We'd like you to be in the church play, Peter. But we don't want you to hit people. Can you promise not to hit people."

"No," said Peter. I'd never heard such sadness in a child's voice. "No, because I just start hitting when I get something like a stick in my hand."

"Peter," I said. "Maybe I can help. I'll sit right in the front row during the Christmas concert. And when you feel like hitting somebody with your shepherd's staff, you just look at me. And then we'll both pretend that I'm giving you a nice, warm hug. Do you think that would work?"

Peter and I exchanged knowing glances several times during the performance. And he got through the Christmas concert just fine.

On the way home, it came to me. I've been playing God! God doesn't zap with thunderbolts or force people into decisions. God simply offers love, in all sorts of forms. Christmas, Good Friday and Easter are at the top of the list.

And then God sits there, in the front row of our lives, smiling and encouraging and helping us find the internal strength to do the right thing.

Christmas is there to remind us to play God – to express love, especially to people who find it hard to receive love, and be there with them through the tough times.

We're called to play God, so they and we may live.

TALENT

Childhood
Gifts
Growth   Matthew 25:14-29
Identity   Luke 19:11-26

Writing a book on men's issues (*Man to Man*) and developing a kit on the subject for use in men's groups, has had some interesting by-products.

I found myself reflecting on my boyhood, and wondering what kind of man had grown out of that boy.

You see, as I boy, I was not in any sense "popular." The fact that my dad was the school principal didn't help a lot. I grew too fast (my nickname changed from Slug to Slim) and my mind no longer knew the length of my limbs. I developed a stoop, which I still have, trying to get down to the size of my school mates. I was the most awkward kid in town. Whenever they chose teams to play anything, I was always chosen last.

I was convinced I had no talent to invest in anything. Thirteen years old and already a failure. So I spent hours in my room writing poems and stories. My mom liked my stories.

"You've got talent," she said. What did she know?

In grade eleven, Miss Thompson, my English teacher liked my stories and my essays. And I got an A+ in English which qualified me as a genuine "twerp." ("Nerd" was not in our vocabulary at that time.)

That was almost half a century ago. Now my classmates are in various states of decrepitude (as I am) and their athletic abilities disappeared with their waistlines. But I get more of a kick out of my writing than ever, and I think I'm even a bit better at it.

There's an old creation legend that the birds felt they'd been had when they looked at their wings.

"What can you do with these things?" they asked God. "You can't walk with them. You can't pick things up. And they're ugly and awkward to carry around."

"You can fly," said God.

"Fly? Waddya mean, fly? What's fly?" the birds demanded.

"Spread them out as wide as you can. Way out wide. Now move them up and down. Harder. Now see, they lift you from the ground. You can fly!"

"Whee!" chirped the birds. "We can fly! Look at us! We can fly! Thanks God! Thanks!"

TELEVISION
Listening
Nourishment   Matthew 7:9
Story   Luke 11:11

We can't survive without stories. But my kids don't know how to crack sunflower seeds, at least not as well as my Uncle Henry, and they don't know how to tell or hear stories very well either. The storyteller in our household has a 23 inch color screen and several channels all of which say much the same thing. This electronic grandmother is telling powerful stories in enticing ways.

That electronic grandmother is a real problem for me. I was a TV producer by profession, and I've got a love-hate relationship going with that medium. Its power is so fantastic; its programing often is so impoverished.

Television is of course, only one of the media that soaks up our stories like a sponge and feeds them back to us. Many magazines, comic books, pocket books, films and other media that exist primarily to make money, do much the same thing.

And when the stories are fed back to us, they're predigested with most of the vitamins removed. All that's left is fat and flavoring.

TELEVISION
Paradox   Matthew 7:9   Luke 11:11

I lived in the province of Alberta for almost a decade. The "land of milk and money" some people called it. Alberta is blessed with lots of oil, lots of beef and lots of money. It has the highest number of cars per capita in Canada, the highest per capita saturation of color TV sets and people hooked up to cable TV.

It also has one of the highest divorce and alcoholism rates. Is there a connection?

TELEVISION

Loneliness
Narcotic
Pain   Matthew 7:9
Worthlessness   Luke 11:11

I don't think TV is the disease attacking our society, but I think it provides the "Dream Whip" culture in which the bacteria grows and spreads. It's such a painless way to die. A drug trip. A narcotic that first dulls the pain of loneliness and worthlessness, then offers us an electronic fantasy through which we can leave real life behind. At least for awhile.

TELEVISION

Imagination
Radio   John 11:35

I first heard a radio broadcast about 55 years ago. I can't remember what it was, except there was a woman crying. In the years that followed, the theater of my mind imagined the setting and detail of thousands of radio dramas from *The Lone Ranger* through *Fibber Magee and Molly* and Lux Radio Theater.

Radio provided a kind of audio-outline of the stories it told; I filled in all the color and detail, the tastes and smells, and, most of all, the feelings, from my own imagination. So the stage for Lux Radio Theater was the world of my small prairie town.

That world was stretched by radio, but never destroyed.

I saw television for the first time after I had already entered the media world as a radio announcer. The very first program I saw was *Ed Sullivan*. Suddenly, I was robbed of my contribution to the media event.

Television could only stretch my imagination up to 21 inches. Instead of Ralph shaping the stories on the media, the media stories were shaping Ralph.

Of course, I didn't recognize it at the time. Everybody thought television was a wonderful new "advance," it gave us a "window on the world."

It certainly is a window, but a very narrow one, with badly distorting glass, and you can't see more than a bit of the horizon.

THANKSGIVING
Birth
Fear
Grandparents
Hope
Joy
Rejoicing   Isaiah 9:6

The phone call came at 12:30 in the morning, after Bev and I had been asleep for a couple of hours. "Hi Grampa," said the voice. It was Don, my son-in-law. "You have a grandson named Jacob Daniel."

Bev and I have a grandson! Unto us a child is born. Unto us a grandson is given. And the government shall be upon his shoulder, and the shoulders of his generation. And his name shall be called Wonderful! Counselor!

Poor kid!

There we were, Bev and I, lying on our bed in the dark, crying and laughing and praying and rejoicing and grieving and knowing it would be a long time before we could get back to sleep.

It was a high and holy time for us. We were welcoming Jacob Daniel in the name of Christ. What is doing anything in the name of Christ, if it is not something you do with every conceivable human emotion, with all your senses tingling, with all your fears and with all your hopes, with all that has been (Thanks!) and for all that will be (Yes!).

And welcoming Jacob Daniel into our midst we of course welcomed the Christ into our midst, as the Christ is always there with every baby born into this painful, suffering, hating, struggling, cruel world.

This evening, Bev and I will go to visit Jacob Daniel and his mom and dad, and I know I will hold in my arms the most beautiful child in all creation, and I will be able to declare it with 100% certainty.

Christ has died! Christ has risen! Christ has come again!

THANKSGIVING

Aboriginal
Celebration
Forgiveness
Healing
Indians
Land
Reflection
Repentance   Deuteronomy 8:7-19

It was your traditional, small-town church Thanksgiving service. The chancel steps were so loaded with corn and potatoes and apples that Bev (my wife who was the minister there at the time) could hardly find her way to the pulpit.

Dominating the whole thing was a pumpkin. A huge pumpkin. It needed three sturdy souls to get it from garden to chancel. We didn't weigh it, but it was 4 1/2 feet in diameter. I had grown it in my compost heap, feeding it, watering, pruning away competing pumpkins. Growing good food from the decaying refuse of our lives has been a life-giving metaphor for me.

After the service, I gave the pumpkin to children from a family that had just broken apart. The delight in the children's eyes, the happiness in their mother's eyes who said, "This is exactly what we need to get us through Thanksgiving" – who could imagine a richer reward?

I love these celebrations. And yet, I always have trouble with Thanksgiving. It's too easy.

It's too easy to get maudlin and sentimental and forget the cost of our circle of plenty.

In Canada, Thanksgiving and Columbus Day happen at the same time. And it would be callous and irresponsible to give thanks for the cornucopia of plenty piled in our chancels, if we did not also ask, "Who owns the land on which these were grown?"

So Thanksgiving must begin with reflection. With repentance. With healing and forgiveness.

Our Thanksgiving is a sham unless we say to ourselves and our politicians, "Mistakes were made. People were robbed of their heritage. What are we going to do about it?"

In the compost of our less than glorious history, we can, with care and hard work, grow fruit that will bring joy to broken hearts.

THANKSGIVING
Denial
Joy
Pain   Luke 2:25-32

I was at a wedding a few weeks ago.

The couple was radiantly happy. There were prayers of thanksgiving in the service, there were speeches and toasts at the reception, all of them delighting in the celebration of a covenant.

At the wedding was the groom's older sister. Her marriage had come apart a few weeks earlier. I caught a glimpse of tears in her eyes during the reception, and because we had been friends for many years, I asked her for a dance and wondered out loud how she was making out. "Does it seem a little unfair?" I asked.

The question surprised her. "No. Not unfair. It's painful, of course. But it's not unfair. In fact, I can rejoice with my brother at a deeper level because I also know the flip side of all this."

I have problems every Thanksgiving when the chancel of our church is loaded with garden produce. I have problems because I'm not convinced garden produce is a suitable symbol any longer. It has more to do with nostalgia than with thanksgiving.

I have problems because so much of secular thanksgiving has to do with denying pain rather than genuine thanksgiving which always takes place in the context of pain.

Earlier in the year, I blubbered all through the wedding of my daughter Kari. I cried with joy, of course, but I also cried because I know the pain and the struggle and the heartache they will have to face if their relationship is to be genuine and life-giving.

When old Simeon held the infant Jesus in the Temple, he told Mary that a "sword will pierce your heart." Old Simeon couldn't predict the future. He could have said that to any mother. Every parent knows that children bring both joy and pain.

In fact, one may not be possible without the other. Easter was not possible without Good Friday.

So with or without pumpkins in front of the pulpit, we are called to be thankful. We are also called to express our pain and our anger and our frustration.

But let's not try to do all of it on one Sunday.

TRADITION

Heaven
Liberalism
Mainstream
Metaphor

Right at the moment, my concept of heaven is a place where there are nice, neat, tidy answers to everything. (As you may guess, my vision of heaven changes, depending on what is bugging me at the moment.)

I have been immeasurably blessed by the lives that have touched mine. I've traveled broadly and lived in three different countries and met good folk from just about every religious tradition going. And I would argue strongly that the Spirit is active in their lives – that they are living an authentic spirituality, often far more authentic than my no-name Protestant Christianity.

On the other hand, my children have very few traditions. Bev and I blended (and I guess watered down) our traditions when we married. And our children, like most children in the developed world, blended those traditions with all they saw and heard from the world around them. My accommodating liberal attitude toward various faith traditions infected my children.

So the underlying but unmistakable message they heard was, "It's all relative. None of it is really that important."

Our traditions are the metaphors through which we communicate our identity and our faith, especially to young children who see what we do and hardly ever hear what we say. They sense immediately when those traditions rest very lightly on our shoulders. They know whether or not we're ready to go to the wall for them.

TRANSFIGURATION

Comfort		Mark 9:2-8
Mother		Luke 9:28-36
Nourishment	Matthew 17:1-8	2 Peter 1:16-18

We were riding on a bus through the Galilee.

Don, our course director, had just pointed out an interesting feature of Mt. Tabor, which is traditionally, the Mount of the Transfiguration. We had just come down from that mountain, and the hot afternoon haze made the mountain shimmer.

We were not tourists. We were a group of students, most of them priests of the Roman Catholic church, a few seminarians, and three laypeople, a nun, a professor of communications and myself. And we had read the scriptures and talked about the transfiguration all the way from our camp on the Sea of Galilee.

We had said a mass in the church at the top of the mountain and heard a homily on the Transfiguration. Then we walked around the top of that mountain and tried to imagine what might have transpired there.

"Did you notice," said Don. "The mountain is shaped like a woman's breast."

It was, very clearly.

I found Don's comment deeply moving. "That brings it together for me," I said. "Jesus returns to his mother God for comfort and nourishment."

The comment was troublesome to most on the bus – deeply offensive to a few. And the conversation quickly came to an embarrassed halt. Little was said till we reached our camp.

The nun took my arm as we got off the bus. "Yes!" she whispered in my ear. "Yes! Yes!"

TRANSFORMATION
Chosen
Communion
Encouragement
Perception
Potential
Recognition
Worth   Matthew 16:17-18

"A silk purse out of a sow's ear." You could, in a sense, sum up the Bible with that old saying.

It's certainly the story of Peter. An illiterate laborer who had never been more than five miles from home, and who believed that was the way it should be.

A sow's ear. Drab. Worthless.

Jesus saw a silk purse.

No, Jesus did not change Peter into something else, Jesus simply recognized the real Peter. And then helped Peter to recognize that too.

That's the story of the whole Bible. God looked at a tiny, dim-witted group of wandering shepherds, led by bigoted, narrow-minded chieftains, and saw a chosen people, a people of destiny, a people who could live a holy covenant.

When we baptize a baby or an adult, we don't change a sow's ear into a silk purse. We celebrate the fact that God sees a silk purse. We celebrate and recognize what God celebrates and recognizes.

We all feel like Peter. Dumb. Grumpy. Not worth much. God is like a new mother with a brand new baby. She looks at the tiny, red, screwed up face and sees a precious being of exquisite beauty. The baby bawls its head of, but the mother hears the song of an angel.

In an awkward kind of way we celebrate that reality every time we gather for communion. It is very ordinary bread we eat, and the stuff we drink is not what they serve in the best restaurants. And we don't turn it, magically, into something more than that. But if we can believe, even if we can believe just a little, that ordinary stuff can nourish us in a way that no *chef de cuisine* could ever hope to do.

Peter saw himself as a sow's ear. I generally see myself as a sow's ear. Every one of us feels like a sow's ear sometimes.

God sees a silk purse.

TRUST
Children
Innocence
Vulnerability   Matthew 18:1-4

I have a friend named MacKenzie. She is six months old and that's her first name. Don't ask me why.

Last night, after MacKenzie had been fed, I held her on my knee for awhile. Naturally, she burped a bit of dinner onto my shirt. Her mother apologized but MacKenzie smiled and bubbled and stiffened her feet to stand up on my lap.

MacKenzie trusts me. She shouldn't of course, because I am not a very reliable person. I've let lots of people down and will probably let her down someday. But she trusts me because she is only six months old and has no alternative.

I am a little older than MacKenzie and I have alternatives. I don't trust everyone the way MacKenzie does. I trust MacKenzie, but then what can she do to me besides spit up on my shirt.

Former US President Lyndon Johnson is quoted as saying he

never trusted anyone unless he had that person's career in his pocket. Johnson did not understand the meaning of the word "trust." Trust is not mutual fear.

My friend Jim Taylor once talked about a person who "I disagree with on many things, but I trust implicitly." I trust Jim, come to think of it, even though I know he will probably forget the lunch date we have on Wednesday. I don't trust him to make all the right decisions or to remember everything or to never let me down on anything. But I trust him. I trust him because I believe him to be a good person, and that he would not take advantage of my vulnerabilities. I am not afraid of Jim.

Maybe that's the same kind of trust I receive from little MacKenzie. Does she know that I will not take advantage of her vulnerabilities? Do I know that?

Perhaps we never really know whom we trust, whom we can trust, till we are laid out on a hospital bed, or broke or in jail or in a nursing home.

Perhaps God can't trust us with the gift of love until then either. Isn't it interesting how Jesus' metaphor of becoming "like a child" keeps coming back to us?

UNITED CHURCH OF CANADA

Conservatism
Diversity
Insight
Liberalism
Majority
Schism

The United Church of Canada was conceived on the windswept prairies where the population was so sparse it was a case of one church or no church at all. Often, these community churches included Catholics, Baptists, Lutherans, as well as the three that finally tied the knot; Methodists, Presbyterians (at least most of them) and Congregationalists. A few years ago, the Evangelical United Brethren joined the family.

The amazing thing, for me, is that this church is still united. Still, the danger of disintegration is far from past, and any healing insights available must be explored, not just for the sake of that church, but for Christians who have similar problems in other denominations. I believe the concept of story telling is one of those insights, though certainly not the only one.

There is much diversity in the United Church, but the danger point is the liberal/conservative split, sometimes visible when we talk about things related to evangelism or the social gospel. Unfortunately, clergy and leading lay people tend to be in the liberal/social-gospel end, while the average lay person is more often in the conservative/evangelistic wing. Having worked closely with churches of many denominations in the US and Canada for twenty years, I'd say that's true of most of them.

While the laity are the majority, theirs is not the voice heard in the courts of the church, and there is considerable resentment of that fact. Unless there is a bridging of that gap, the laity will simply and quietly withdraw their support and drift into churches where they see more of themselves in the public pronouncements.

No group within any church has a monopoly on myopia.

The sophisticated thinly-disguised patronizing disdain of the liberal/social-gospel group is matched by the self-righteous dogmatism of the conservative/evangelical wing.

I'm well aware that genuine differences in theology do exist, and I'm not suggesting they be ignored. In addition, there are emotional differences between people; some folks respond to one type of religious style and others respond to another. On top of all that are ethnic, economic, social, historical and educational factors.

UNITY
Diversity
Flexibility
Harmony
Law
Love
Strength   2 Corinthians 12

When people rode around in wagons, and in the early days of automobiles, they sometimes used steel tires.

Steel tires had many good points. They kept the wooden wheel from falling apart on the bumpy dirt and gravel roads. Often the steel wheels outlasted the wagon and the car. And nobody ever had a flat tire.

But steel wheels were mighty hard on the passengers. It was a bone jarring ride. So somebody invented the rubber tire, then the pneumatic tire, and the passengers loved it.

Except when they had to get out and fix a flat. That happened often. Steel tires were hard and inflexible. But they lasted. Rubber tires were soft and pliable. But they wore out quickly.

Then somebody had a brain wave. Why not find a way to combine the strength of steel with the softness of rubber? The result was the steel-belted radial.

And not a bad metaphor to explain God's law and God's love. Safe. Soft. And long-lasting.

VALUES
Changes
Complacency
Despair
Development
Ecology
Journey
Nuclear Threat
Pessimism
Progress
War   Romans 8:18-26

In Moscow, the crowds have pulled down the statue of Lenin. Lenin was the great saint of communist ideology.

Nature abhors a vacuum, ideological or otherwise, so Moscow now has a new icon. McDonald's golden arches.

Has anything really changed?

The Cold War cost the world a trillion dollars a year. Now the Cold War is over, the USSR doesn't exist anymore, and NATO is trying to justify itself.

Has there been a peace dividend? Instead of the cold war, we've had an escalation of the trade in arms. As many, if not more guns and bombs are being built, sucking the life from innocent children.

Has anything really changed?

No.

But also, yes.

The revolution from the Czars to Lenin began with "Bloody Sunday" in 1905 with the massacre of 1,500 innocent people. The revolution from Lenin to Ronald McDonald was accomplished with few fatalities. It's still the politics of power, but gradually, slowly, people are learning how to assert themselves without violence.

The threat of nuclear disaster began with the massacre of innocent people in Hiroshima and Nagasaki. At that time, it didn't occur to me or to most people what a horrifying thing that was.

But in the Iraq war, the US had to at least pretend there were no civilian casualties. Dropping an A-bomb on Iraq would have been politically unthinkable.

A few months ago, a huge international conference on the ecology was held in Rio de Janeiro, attended by the world's most powerful politicians. It didn't accomplish much, but it put ecological concerns firmly on the world agenda. Ten years ago, only a few eco-freaks thought about those kinds of things.

You can say with justification that nothing has changed. There's been no progress! The old values are still in place. We're still ruled by the politics of greed. That's mostly what we hear from our "prophetic" church leadership.

It's half-truth and half-lie.

My temptation on hearing such knee-jerk pessimism is to retreat into thumb-sucking despair. If we've made no progress, what arrogance leads us to believe our efforts are going to make any difference in the future? Why bother?

But I'm old enough to look back over my shoulder. At a writer's event with novelist Madeleine L'Engle recently, I challenged her on a statement she'd made in one of her books about inclusive language. "Ralph, that book was written 12 years ago," she said. "I've moved." All of us have moved. I remember what worried us half a century ago. I can read my own writings of four decades ago and see how far I've moved. I'm convinced that in my lifetime, the world – all of the world – has moved a long, long way.

I'm also young enough to look ahead to see how very, very far we still have to go. The world is still enslaved by power and greed, and with our increased awareness of that goes the responsibility to keep pushing. Hard.

Chronic pessimism leads to despair. Mindless optimism leads to complacency. Neither is prophetic.

The Hebrews and the early Christian church often felt the raw winds of despair and the seductive winds of complacency. They looked back to where they had been and how God had been part of that. And from in their remembering found hope and heard themselves called to live out God's future.

We, as Christians, can look back over our own short lifetimes and see where we have been, and where God has been a part of our journey.

We rejoice in how far God has moved us. And from our celebration of God active in our past, we draw strength to hear God's call to our future.

VANITY

Clothing	Matthew 6:25
Fashion	Luke 12:22
Style	Romans 12:2

The Chinese used to practice foot binding. We still practice neck binding. And ours is supposed to be an advanced culture.

I mean why, for heaven's sake, would anyone ever wear a tie? Why would any half-way rational intelligent male voluntarily subject himself to this ancient instrument of torture? Maybe we've cut the circulation off from our heads for so long, our brains have shriveled like a Japanese orange in January. We can't think anymore.

A tie has absolutely no function except to clean eye glasses and it doesn't even do that well. It just smears the muck around. It makes about as much sense as those grenade loops we used to have on trench coats. Maybe even less, because the guy with the trench coat could at least carry grenades if he happened to be a revolutionary. What can you do with a tie?

It doesn't impress anybody. Nobody even notices, unless you wear one so bilious you can hear it a block away. Then people just pretend they don't know you. I was with a guy in Toronto once who couldn't get into a restaurant because he wasn't wearing a tie. He went into the men's toilet, pulled a lace from his shoe, put it around his turtleneck sweater, and they let him in.

The only males allowed into restaurants like that (of which, thankfully, there are few) without a tie are clergy. That is, they can get in without a tie if they wear an even more ridiculous alternative, a stiff Roman collar. The clerical collar (for the benefit of lay people) is a miniature neck brace, which not only cuts off circulation to the head but makes it impossible to nod, thus keeping the poor preacher from saying "yes" to anything that might be fun.

And ours is supposed to be an advanced culture!

VARIETY

Covenant
Creation
Diversity
Hope
Promise
Rainbow   Genesis 9:13-17

There's no such thing as a one-color rainbow. The rainbow has every color of the universe. Every subtle shade of every hue is there.

There's an old, old story in the Bible about Noah. God had given up on the world and decided to start all over. A worldwide flood would wipe everything out. Only a few would be saved, like a bit of yeast, to start things all over again.

Near the end of the story, God is having second thoughts. God realizes that destroying creation is not the way to solve a problem, and God promises not to do that again.

Then God makes a promise, to all creation. To every living thing. To every creature and every plant. And the symbol of that promise is God's crazy upside-down smile across the whole sky, a rainbow, a glorious, shining spectrum of all the colors of the universe, even colors we humans can't see.

And in God's promise is a call to the only creatures that are created in God's image. We, the human race, are called to love that whole spectrum of creation, in all its wonderful diversity, in all its infinite variety. Because we are created in that divine image, that rainbow smile is our smile and God's smile, that rainbow smile is our sure hope that the power of God is in the love of creation, and that God's hope rests with those of us within creation who share the rainbow smile.

VIOLENCE

Death
Depersonalization
Justice
Television   Judges 16:28-30
Tragedy   Judges 19, 20

About a year ago, I saw a performance of *Hamlet*. The final curtain fell on a stage strewn with corpses. A few days earlier I had been writing a speech about violence on TV. So I wondered, in what way was "Hamlet" different from "Today's FBI" or "MacLean's Law" or any other police-detective program? Besides, isn't violence a part of human nature? Yes, it is.

But if you check with your local police department, you'll find that most murderers kill family members, friends or lovers. The death is a tragedy for everyone, including the killer, regardless of what course the law takes.

"Hamlet" was like that. In the fullest sense, the killings were a tragedy, for the King who was the villain, for Hamlet the hero, and for the audience. It was an all-around "no-win" situation, like violence in real life.

Popular TV dramas that deal in violence are fundamentally different. Most of the people murdered (about 70 percent) are anonymous. The initial murder that triggers the plot is of an undeveloped character; someone who has been on the screen only a few seconds (perhaps not at all) before being killed. Often all you see is the feet of the corpse behind the sofa. So it's hardly a tragedy. You haven't had a chance to identify with the character in any sense, so you don't take the death personally.

Most of the deaths you actually see happen on TV are of bad guys, and almost invariably males; it's the villain gunned down by Starsky or MacLean in the final minutes of the plot.

But that's not tragic either, because the bad guy got it. Justice is done!

There are a few, but not many, deaths portrayed on TV which show real people; deaths which are tragic and personal.

But they're the exception. Most TV deaths are depersonalized.

It's not real people we see dying, just nobodies and bad guys.

VIOLENCE

Commitment
Fear
Relationships
Television
Value

I've been reading a bit of research data lately, and it seems there's one thing we know for sure about people who watch a lot of physical violence on TV. They get scared. They are more afraid of being hurt physically than people who don't watch a lot of media mayhem. So they stay indoors more, away from possible injury.

Doesn't it stand to reason that people who continually see others being put down; being used as sex objects rather than being loved as persons; being told implicitly by advertisers that their only value is in what they buy; seeing no deep long-term loving relationships but only temporary alliances; wouldn't those people become a little wary of making commitments to other human beings?

Is TV perhaps the virus that infects our world with the disease of loneliness?

VOCATION
Call
Ministry   Exodus 3:10-12

We didn't go up the mountain.

There were three of us, all with the same ailment. Knees that hurt, and could not have handled the hike up to the top of Mt. Sinai. The rest of our study group went with our instructor to the top, where they would talk about Moses, live themselves into that theophany, and take the time to pray and thank God for the gift of law.

We waited down below, a Lutheran professor, a Roman Catholic nun and I, and we felt a bit of anger at our knees for failing us, when we wanted so much to go up that mountain to remember Moses and the Ten Commandments.

The ugly hulk of St. Catherine's Monastery hunkered down just below us. Just above, the caves of countless generations of monks who came to pray their lives out in this desolation. "Why?" I wondered. "Why would anyone want to do such a thing? I couldn't imagine spending a night in such a place, much less half a lifetime."

"There must have been a call," said the nun.

"Tell me about 'call'," I asked. "Protestants don't know much about that."

I was wrong. The Lutheran professor did. He had a deep, powerful sense that God called him to a vocation of teaching, of drawing creativity into the lives of students. And the nun too, but her call was to be a really good administrator at her convent.

"If you really stop and listen," said the nun, "God tells you. Go. Do. It's really not very complicated."

The shadows gathered round the Moses mountain and our group

came straggling down the slopes. They walked in silence.

Clyde, a youthful seminarian came to me and placed a small red rock into my hand. "I brought this down for you," he said. "I'm sorry you couldn't come."

"Thanks," I said. "How was it?"

His eyes filled with tears. "It's just another mountain," he said. "But you know, the stones up top are worn smooth by the knees of people praying there. And I really could hear God talk to me up there. I didn't hear words. But I knew, with everything I was, that God was the source of power and love, and that I was being called into that ministry."

"I know," I said. "I could hear it all the way down here."

VOLUNTEERS

Aging
Altruism
Caring
Giving
Love
Service   John 5:20, 14:12

After my Dad died, Mom needed a job. She needed a job for the money, but she also needed to do something with herself. Time was heavy on her hands.

She got a job at the School for Deaf Children near Winnipeg. The school is closed now, and the children integrated into the regular school system, but at that time there were about a hundred children of varying ages, all of whom were deaf.

Mom was in charge of the laundry. Sheets, pillowcases, towels, that sort of thing. But she fell in love with the children, and when the laundry duties were done, she would stay on and spend time with them.

"What do you do with the kids?" I asked. "Do you teach them things?"

"No," she said. "Sometimes I read to them."

"But I thought they were deaf."

"They are. But they want a lap to sit on. They just need somebody to hold them for awhile. Kids need to be loved. And they seem to enjoy the feel of my voice, even if they can't hear it."

Mom learned how to sign – this when she was well past 60 – so she could communicate more easily. And most days, when her laundry work was finished at 5:00, she would stay on with the children till they were all safely tucked into bed.

When government regulations required Mom to retire at age 65 she got permission to keep coming back to the school. So for years, until her health began to fail, Mom spent her days with the youngsters at the School for Deaf Children.

"Why don't you take it easy, Mom?" I would ask from time to time.

"Because I enjoy it," she would say. "Those children are wonderful. They keep me young. They need me."

My mother is like thousands of other volunteers, many of them retired, who give and receive life as they reach out in love to others. And in their giving, they receive.

When Jesus talked about "greater works" that we might do, I think that's one of the things he had in mind.

WISDOM

Aging
Beginnings
Call
Challenge
Fear
Fulfillment
Hope   2 Corinthians 4:16-18
Promise   James 1:5

There's a wonderful cartoon showing a very concerned man beside a very pregnant woman. She is being wheeled into the delivery room. He leans over and says, "Now dear, are you sure you want to go through with this?"

I think I know how the woman on her way into the delivery room felt. Old age begins at birth. At first there's excitement and challenge and accomplishment, but in the final stages, there is a voice saying, "Do I really want to go through with this?" To which the answer is a question: "Do I have a choice?"

As I get older, I'm tempted to feel anger and despair because nothing in the old body works quite as well. But at the same time, I sense the birth of something I might be arrogant enough to call "wisdom" which is not at all like being smart.

Once you head into that delivery room, there is no coming back. Once you launch a new life, there is no coming back. Growing old or being born is frightening – uncertain. Cataclysmic. Inevitable. But if we let it, also hopeful.

God's call into the new and peaceable kingdom is all that and more. Like Jesus, we don't know exactly how those cataclysmic events will occur, or when. All we know is that we're being wheeled into the delivery room. And nothing will ever be the same again.

Once more, God's ancient promise is fulfilled.

WORK
Computers
Prayer
Vocation   Luke 10:38-42

It was one of those questions encountered on an airplane. A fellow passenger asked me, "So, what do you do for a living?"

"I'm a writer."

"So, what do you write?"

"Materials for clergy. For the churches."

"Are you religious?"

I'm always tempted to lie at that point, because I'm afraid of red-eyed fundamentalists and hollow-eyed atheists who can make a five hour flight seem like several days. Sometimes I'm evasive, but I don't usually lie.

"Well, no," I said. "Not in the usual sense. Not in the sense in which the media tend to use that word."

"That's good," he said. And buried himself in a newspaper. But I thought about his question for the next hour or so.

A more honest response would have been, "Yes, I'm religious. Yes, very." And I might have added that I am religious because I'm a writer. Writing is my prayer life.

Except for church, I don't have a prayer time. But I often sit down at my computer and start to type something – a letter, an article – and my fingers seem to take off. I find myself typing hard and fast and sometimes hardly believing what appears on my screen. I have confessed to things, had insights and revelations and felt passions that couldn't possibly have come just from my own head.

I've tried praying without a keyboard and mostly fallen asleep or found my mind wandering. But like Martha, it's when I do what I call work, that God seems to break in.

WORSHIP
Clergy
Spiritual Starvation
Wilderness   Mark 6:30-32

At a gathering of clergy some years back for a workshop on hospital chaplaincy, the question was raised, "When you lead in worship, do you also worship?"

Most of the clergy said, "No."

I found that very upsetting. Most of my close friends are clergy and the thought that they may be denied what I find so life-giving, was deeply disturbing to me.

I sense some of the reasons. While I'm a layperson, I get called to preach or lead in worship more than most laypeople. While I enjoy the preaching, I do not like being worship leader. My mind is far too preoccupied with all the details of leading in worship to allow me to worship at the same time. And so when I get to the preaching, it suffers. You can't preach well when you're hungry.

I have no idea what to do about that, and I certainly don't intend this as yet another guilt-trip to lay on the clergy.

My worship life, and I'm talking about the regular Sunday gathering of my congregation, gives me life and hope and direction.

I receive food for my journey. In our communion service, we symbolically serve and feed each other. But is the pastor who leads the service also fed?

Numbered among the starving people of the world, should we include our clergy?

SUBJECT INDEX

A

aboriginal 167
acceptance 90
achievement 11, 132
action 82, 138
activism 147
Adam 64
ADVENT 7
advent 104
ADVERTISING 8
AFFIRMATION 8
aging 180, 181
AIDS 10, 82
airplanes 47, 49
altruism 180
ancestors 67
ANDERSON, MARION 11
anger 52, 56
apocalyptic 102
appreciation 77
art 96
ASSUMPTIONS 11
assumptions 35, 36
ATTENDANCE 12
attendance 125, 149
attentiveness 138
ATTITUDE 13
attitude
    8, 81, 82, 88, 91, 92, 113, 145
attitude toward clergy 33
attitudes 70
audience 143
AUTHENTICITY 13
authenticity 12, 85
awareness 59, 64, 138

B

baptism 77, 153
basics 20
beauty 159
beginnings 181
BELIEF 17
belief 85
belonging 70
Bethlehem 27
Bible 67, 98
BIBLE, INTERPRETATION OF 19
Bible, interpretation of 18
BIBLE STUDY 18
Bible study 80
birth 78, 117, 166

blessedness 117
blessing 117, 158
blindness 72
born again 46, 59, 72
BREAD 20
bread, breaking of 40
brothers 117

C

CALL 21
call 56, 128, 179, 181
cancer 76
caring 25, 180
celebration 167
ceremony 153
challenge 101, 181
changes 174
character 107
CHARISMATIC 22
charismatic 38, 145
cheap grace 154
childhood 162
CHILDREN 23
children
    9, 16, 59, 80, 84, 103, 151,
        152, 171
CHILDREN'S STORIES IN
    CHURCH 24
choice 78, 104, 127, 136
chosen 30, 102, 170
CHRISTMAS 24, 25, 26, 28, 30
Christmas 78
Christmas narratives **160**
Christology 17, 103
church 84, 89, 92
church attendance 125
CHURCH CONFERENCES 31
citizenship 15
civil rights 56, 147
CLERGY 33
clergy 108, 143, 144, 145, 183
CLERGY, FEMALE 34, 35, 36
clergy, female 33
clothing 176
CLOWNS 37
clowns 89, 93
comfort 20, 169
commitment 61, 125, 178
communes 42

Sermon
Seasonings

187

BIBLICAL INDEX

Sermon
Seasonings

191